大展好書　好書大展
品嘗好書　冠群可期

大展好書　好書大展

品嘗好書．冠群可期

中英文對照武學 9

盧式心意六合拳入門

附VCD

Lu Style Xinyi Liuhe Quan for Beginners

余江 著
Author Jiang Yu

孫慧敏 姜淑霞 翻譯
Translated by Huimin Sun, Shuxia Jiang

大展出版社有限公司

感　謝

　　這一套介紹盧式心意六合拳的書雖然由我執筆完稿，實來是集體智慧的結晶，一是繼承王書文老師及前輩們經驗的傳授，二是這些年與眾師兄弟們無間交流的成果，書中的某些段落文字還仗著有宿琳、王周、吳秋亭、譚全勝老師們的無私提供。

　　感謝盧少君師叔在病危中爲本書提詞。感謝這些年常在一道打拳、喝茶的蔡泊澄、薛鴻恩、李傳鄉、錢仁表、唐毓堃、張岳定、孫雙喜等師兄們。感謝遠在加拿大的胡剛兄百忙中爲本書寫序。

余　江

盧式心意六合拳入門

Special Thanks

Although this book was finished a piece of writing by me to introduce Lu Style Xinyi Liuhe Quan, actually it was a collective intelligence, one part came from Master Shuwen Wang and many predecessors'impart, the other is the result of interflow between me and many fellow apprentices of one and the same master, some words in this book were provided selflessly by Master Lin Su, Master Zhou Wang, Master Qiuting Wu, and Master Quansheng Tan.

I special appreciate for Master Shaojun Lu writes the inscription when he was critically ill. And many thanks for Bocheng Cai, Hongen Xue, Chuanxiang Li, Renbiao Qian, Yukun Tang, Yueding Zhang, Shuangxi Sun. They practice with me frequently in these years. Thanks Gang Hu in Canada wrote me the preface although he is very busy.

Jiang Yu

一代宗師盧嵩高像
The picture of Master Songgao Lu

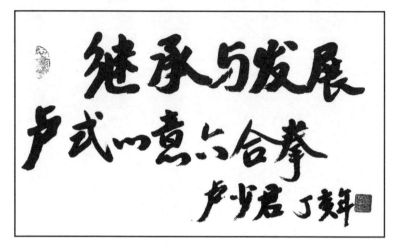

Inheritance and development Lu Style Xinyi Liuhe Quan
Shaojun Lu

註：盧少君老師爲盧嵩高之子

Note: Master Shaojun Lu is the son of Songgao Lu

為盧式心意著作序

中華文化博大精深，絕非虛語。其一爲文，其二曰武，其三不計其數。

文之證據：

三墳、五典、八索、九丘、詩經、諸子、楚辭、漢賦、樂府、唐詩、宋詞、元曲、明清小說、民國白話，聖跡無度，一貫法書。

武之實驗：

七經典武，計謀贏輸；千年秦劍，寒光發怵；朝改代換，長城具睹，金戈鐵馬，成敗不素；內外各族，幾度征服；戰例難數，殘陽月渡；英雄輩出，血雨江湖；民間武林，門派奇數；鄉間村落，高手頻步；北少南武，中南山柱；豪傑無數，把把拳術；地球萬載，此景誰住？

回首武林一片，心意六合閃亮武林幾百年。以根源而論，發之於黃河，遠不說宋代岳武穆英雄一世，就明末至清中，姬龍鳳、曹繼武、馬學禮、戴龍邦、金一望各先祖及傳人，躍於黃河兩岸，威風席捲中原

盧式心意六合拳入門

大地一片；民國時期，原傳一支寶鼎，盧嵩高、尚學禮、宋國賓、范百川諸前輩，引其入長江大流域，風起雲湧武林知。以朝代時局論，心意拳演變分支現，竟與中國命運一一大相息！今上海推出盧式心意拳，對應何？原來是華夏文化復興大時機！

六合心意一脈，何至於此，主根不變，支支變，卻與中國命運環環相扣、節節緊密連？蓋其文化之深也！ 何其深？不可深問焉！留於近日見分曉！

蓋其技術之精也！何其精？不可喻也！空口無憑，留待各位去驗體。

武師風範，盧氏諸公，武藝文獻皆傳授，更有拳譜定乾坤，佐證河南山西六合文！

文士雅儒，余江諸位，事業生活兩成功；繼承發展都不誤，分享深度樂趣於社會；忽發好術於此書，按部就班人人知，何其幸？！心意上海幾老：李，王，凌，于諸公在其中！

黃河、長江、海洋大融流，時光匆匆；名利無邊，體有限，留與少許於心意，回報定不已！

勉爲序！

胡剛於加拿大首府渥汰華探微齋

Introduction of Lu Style Xinyi

The Chinese culture is extensive and profound, and includes literary and martial arts.

The example of the martial art : the classic seven books of martial arts (Wu Jin Qi Shu) for wars. The ancient sword made thousands of years ago in Qin Dynasty still shines.

How many dynasties were replaced? The Great Wall knows. The shining spears and armored horses, no matter victorious or defeated, all bled. Some ethnic groups made conquests both within and without.

How many battles were fought? Only the sun and the moon know. Heroes appeared one after another, from the blood competitions in the old times of China.

Many styles of the martial arts exist in Chinese Wushu society. Even in countryside, there are many masters.

The famous martial arts which are related to the mountains are Shaolin (originated from Shong Mountain) in north, Wudang (originated from Wudang Mountain) in South and Xinyi Quan (originated from Zhongnan Mountain) in the middle.

盧式心意六合拳入門

Heroes, who have their own styles of martial arts, are countless. For thousands of years on the earth, who owns these but China?

When you recall the history of martial arts in China, Xinyi Liuhe Quan has shined in the Wushu society for hundreds years.

Xinyi Liuhe Quan originated from the Yellow River. Even without mentioning the Song Dynasty's hero Yue Fei, there are still Master Longfeng Ji, Jiwu Cao, Xueli Ma, Longbang Dai and Yiwang Jing from the Ming Dynasty and in the middle of the Qing Dynasty, as well as other disciples, spread across the nation and known by both sides of the Yellow River, their power and prestige sweeping the Central Plains.

At the beginning of the last century, the masters such as Mr. Songgao Lu, Xueli Shang, Guobin Song, Baichuan Fan etc. brought Xinyi from the Yellow River to the area of Changjiang River (the Yangtse River), and to the attention of everyone in the Chinese martial arts society.

When we trace back, we are surprised to find that the changes in Xinyi Quan reflect many historical changes in China.

What Lu Style Xinyi is reflecting today? It is reflecting the revival of Chinese culture today!

Why does Liuhe Xinyi have this connection to Chinese history? First, it is because the culture is profound. How profound?

為盧式心意著作序

You will discover for yourself very soon. Second, it is that the techniques are excellent. How excellent? There are no words to describe their excellence; the readers will realize through practice.

The styles of Mr. Lu and the other masters have not only taught the techniques, but also left the Quan Pu (book of theory) to their students. For example, the Quan Pu of Liu He Quan left by Master Lu gave a solid foundation to the Shanghai Xinyi, which also proved that the preface in the Liuhe Quan kept in Shanxi is real.

Mr Jiang Yu and others are not only successful in business but also in life; not only have they inherited Xinyi Quan, but they have also improved and shared it with the society.

Today, they will publish the book on Lu Style Xinyi, and how lucky the readers are to follow their steps to learn Lu Style Xinyi!

How lucky the senior masters (over 80 years old) Li, Wang, Lin and Yu are to be involved too!

The Yellow River, Changjiang River, and the oceans are interflowing; time is flying by, fame and fortune are endless, but not life. Why not leave some time to practice Xinyi and be rewarded with a better health?

Preface by Hugang
Ottawa, the capital of Canada

卷首語

一個外國人，想要瞭解中國文化，想要進入中國人的人文精神世界，給你說一個法子，去學習中國的書法或武術。因為他是中國文化中最純粹中國化的。

一個中國人，想要更深刻地感知自己，成就其自己一個中國人，建議你擠出時間來學習書法或武術，因為他是中國文化中最純粹中國化的。

武術、書法是漢文化的最佳外在表現，由外入內，這是最好的法子。

中國的文化是隱性的，似水流蓮，直面它時，就像面對一張大的無法想像邊際的網，一時會張口無言或言不知所云，因為它高人一頭的一切都是隱喻的、意象的。如書法中草書、國畫中的寫意、武術中的心意拳，都是見其形，取其意，重其心有所悟。鬆是意的界，靈是意的魂，所有的機智都是隱藏的，所有的一切也如同陰陽一樣無時無刻不在變化著。

繼而細細想來還是有序可言：如學習書法時，應學先楷書後習草書；學習國畫時，應先學白描後習寫意；學習武術時，應先學象形後習心意，都是要經過入形、入相、入定三個階段。

入形：教什麼習什麼，學什麼是什麼。

入相：腦中要有一幅幅圖像，是前人的或是大自然中的，時時對照，學什麼要像什麼。

入定：定能生慧，想什麼就會什麼。

博大精深是中國文化的形而象，大到你是什麼人，你想要什麼，他就會給你什麼，像《西遊記》中悟空學藝一般。

因人而異、因材施教是教之法；熟能生巧、溫故知新是學之法，鐵杵成針。

盧式心意六合拳入門

Author's preface

As non – Chinese people, if you would like to understand the Chinese culture and enter the spiritual world of Chinese civilization, there is a way: learn China's calligraphy or martial arts because they are the purest forms of Chinese culture.

As someone of Chinese decent, if you want to perceive more about yourself and achieve more in Chinese culture, make time to learn calligraphy or martial arts because they are the purest forms of Chinese culture.

Martial Arts and calligraphy ······ the best manifestations of the Chinese culture, from outside to inside, is the best way to learn Chinese culture.

The Chinese culture is recessive, like ripples on the surfaces of the water. When you first face it, it is like facing a huge, unimaginable, boundless net. You are astonished and speechless and do not know where to start, because it is superior, recessive and not what it seems. Such as the cursive style of writing in calligraphy, the freehand brushwork in traditional Chinese paintings, Xinyi Quan in martial arts – you have to see the appearance and learn the meanings. The most important part is to comprehend it. All the wisdom is contained deeply inside of the soul and thought, and everything is like Yin Yang, which never stops changing.

Only after you think it over carefully can you find the rules and orders to follow. For example, when learning calligraphy, study regular script before cursive style. When learning traditional Chinese painting, start line drawing before freehand brushwork. When learning martial arts, learn by the image first then learn to control by mind. They all have to go through three stages: Imitation, Into the Picture, and Build In.

Imitation: Copy, follow the masters. Learn what is taught.

Into the Picture: There are images in your head of ancestors or nature. Compare constantly. Picture what you have learnt.

Build In: Wisdom, do whatever you want to. Do whatever's on your mind.(to achieve what you want ?)

The Chinese culture is broad and profound. Depending on what kind of a person you are, it will give you whatever you want, like Sun Wu Kong's KongFu in "Journey to the West".

According to the student's ability is the way to teach. Practicing and reviewing is the way to learn. Day by day, time by time one will achieve perfection just like the old saying says that one can make a needle from an iron bar by keeping grinding it.

盧式心意六合拳入門

能文能武一條龍

　　在我們的文化中，文武是核心。能文能武是每一個望子成龍人家的理想，文可安邦，武可定國，對一個人來講，也要有兩手常備無患：文的一手，武的一手，文可如魚得水，武可養延保命。能文能武是每一個中國人完美的人生追求，是成就一番事業所必備的。

　　武文化的核心是流傳千年的俠文化，他所關心的是：大義、公平、良心，是推動中國上下五千年潮起潮落的原動力，在中國文化中他是最具草根性的 —— 愛國、感恩、正氣、大義、誠信……威武不能屈、富貴不能移……他的屬性是和平的、止戈性的，因為我有武之術才能做到「魔高一尺、我高一丈」。武之術捍衛的是：公平、正義。修為的是：良心、勇敢。武之術的品格應是高貴的、有尊嚴的、有德行的。

　　習武之術的人，應是有武之德的人，才有可能成一位能文能武的人—— 受人尊敬、成就一番事業、朋友遍天下。

盧式心意六合拳入門

People who are wise and skilled in both martial arts and academia are like dragons

Academia and martial arts are the heart of the Chinese culture. To let their sons have both is every family's dream. Academia can be used to develop the country. Martial arts can be used to guard the country. People who knew both were like fish in the water. It presented a perfect life and was necessary to accomplish a career.

The culture of the Chinese Martial Arts is righteous, impartial, and conscientious, which has been integral power in promoting China for the past five thousand years, like a tide full of ups and downs. It is the root of the grass in the Chinese culture—patriotic, grateful, healthy trends, righteous, and sincere. ⋯ Never bow to power and be determined no matter poor or rich⋯ Its attributes are peace and antiwar. Only Martial Arts can allow one to achieve: no matter how high an evil power is, my skill is higher by 10 times. Martial Arts represent fairness and righteousness and also helps cultivate oneself according to conscience and bravery. Martial arts should be characterized by moral, honor, and nobility.

People who learn Martial Arts must have the character first, and then to gain both the literary ability wisdom and Martial Arts skills—to win people's respect, to accomplish undertakings, and to make more friends all around the world.

能文能武一條龍

盧式心意六合拳入門

目　錄

盧式心意六合拳入門

Table of Contents

盧式心意・人物

The Elegancy of Lu Style Xinyi
The originator and Masters

岳飛創拳說

拳譜曰：相傳心意拳是南宋抗金名將岳飛所創，用以訓練將士，殺敵報國，故又稱：岳武穆王拳。

岳飛：字鵬舉（1103—1142），尊號：岳武穆。相州湯陰（今屬河南）人。能文能武，戎馬一生，衝鋒陷陣126仗，未嘗一敗，是名副其實的常勝將軍。他是偉大的民族英雄、崇高的愛國主義象徵、大義的榜樣。

《岳飛詩詞·滿江紅》

怒髮衝冠，憑欄處、瀟瀟雨歇。

抬望眼、仰天長嘯，壯懷激烈。

三十功名塵與土，八千里路雲和月。

莫等閒、白了少年頭，空悲切。

靖康恥，猶未雪；臣子恨，何時滅？

駕長車踏破、賀蘭山缺。

壯志饑餐胡虜肉，笑談渴飲匈奴血。

待從頭、收拾舊山河，朝天闕。

Xinyi Quan Creator – Fei Yue

The legend in the specifications of Xinyi Quan says that the Xinyi Quan was created by the Southern Song Dynasty's famous anti-Jin General Fei Yue. He used it to train soldiers and his men to attack the enemies and serve the country. Therefore, it is also called the 'Wu Mu Yue Quan'.

Fei Yue, symbol Ju Peng (1103 –1142), granted name: Wu Mu Yue (equals to a duke in England), born in Tang Yin, Xiang Zhou (now Henan province). He was a high ranking scholar and excellent at Chinese martial arts. He served in the army for his whole life, charged and broke through enemy lines in 126 battles and never lost. He was a true triumphant General. He was a great national hero, a lofty patriotic symbol and a great example of righteousness.

Fei Yue's Poem "River Full of Red"

My wrath bristles through my helmet, the rain stops as I stand by the rail;

I look up towards the sky and let loose a passionate roar.

At age thirty my deeds are nothing but dust, my journey has taken me over eight thousand li [1]

So do not sit by idly, for young men will grow old in regret.

The humiliation of Jing Kang [2] still lingers,

When will the pain of his subjects ever end?

Let us ride our chariots through the Helan Pass,

There we shall feast and drink on barbarian flesh and blood.

Let us begin anew to recover our old empire [3], before paying tribute to the Emperor.

1. One li (ancient Chinese measurement of distance) is about a half of a kilometre or a 1/3 of a mile.

2. This is in reference to the shame of the capture of Kaifeng and Emperor Qinzong in the Jingkang Incident in 1127.

3. In 1141 the Song signed the humiliating Treaty of Shaoxing that forced the Song Dynasty to renounce all claims to all lands north of the Huai river, along with Yue Fei's execution. In other words, the Chinese were humiliated into becoming a tributary of the Jurchens.

Note: The poem is translated by James T. C. Liu. "Yueh Fei (1103–41) and China's Heritage of Loyalty." The Journal of Asian Studies. Vol. 31, No. 2 (Feb., 1972), pp. 291–297. The information comes from Wikipedia, the free encyclopedia,

盧式心意鼻祖**盧嵩高**老師

盧師一生只做一件事——研習武術，開創了中國武術一派之先河，成其了一代宗師的崇高地位。一生守法忠義，守德明理，人格高尚，人生清白，寧守清貧，不事漢奸，具有很強的民族氣節；一生從事傳統武術的傳授、民族文化的傳播，桃李芬芳滿天下。

盧師，河南周口人，生於 1875 年—歸真於 1961 年，回族。自幼習武，十多歲時就拜心意門第七代武術大師袁鳳儀老師為師學習武術，在明師的指點下，二十六歲時已是武藝超群，被河南周口得勝鏢局聘為鏢師。

舊中國世道黑暗，中原地區戰亂頻繁，廣大人民群眾生活在水深火熱之中。盧老師經人介紹從河南輾轉來到上海，短暫的在麵粉商人——陳公館（榮家）中當過保鏢，後來替榮家管理過倉庫。也就是在這一時期，因緣際會結識了心意門第六代弟子中年齡最小的丁仁老師（河南桑坡人，回民，在滬從事皮貨生意，住在五馬路）。丁老師經人介紹知道盧老師在上海傳授心意門功夫，經過多日的觀察後才找到盧師，盧師也早就聽說過這位小師爺，對其十分的敬重。

看過盧老師的功夫後，丁老師說：我現在可以將擔子卸給你了。

在以後半年多的時間裡，盧師每天都到五馬路回民教堂的樓上秘密跟著丁仁老師學習心意六合拳。

盧師一生一直從事武術的研習與傳授，在不斷的實踐、學習、交流中，擁有自己鮮明特點、獨特風格的盧式心意六合拳在20世紀三、四十年代逐漸形成並廣為流傳，開創了中國武術一派之先河。

盧老師是上海心意六合拳的開山鼻祖。

The Earliest Ancestor of Lu Style Xinyi in ShangHai – Master Songgao Lu

Master Lu dedicated his whole life to studying Chinese Martial Arts. He created the first of its kind and achieved a high status in Chinese Martial arts. He was loyal, moral, reasonable, and respectable. He was characterized by his national integrity. He was devoted to teaching Martial Arts and propagating Chinese culture. His students are found all over the country.

Master Lu, born 1875, Zhou Kou, Henan province, died 1961, Muslim. He started to learn Martial Arts when he was very young. At the age of ten, he became a student of Master

Fenyi Yuan, who was of the seventh generation of Xinyi Quan. With this wise teacher guiding, he became outstanding at Chinese Martial Arts. At the age of twenty – six, he was hired to be a guard of De Shen Biao Ju, which is an armed escort agency responsible for guarding all kinds of expensive articles during their transportation.

In old China, the central areas were full of chaos caused by wars. People lived miserable lives. Master Lu struggled with his life and came to Shanghai. He became a bodyguard shortly of a powerful businessman, Chen's residence (Rong family) and then managed their warehouse. At the time, he met Master Ren Ding, the youngest of the 6th generation descendants of Xinyi Quan through Yuan Ji Hua (meeting by fate) (Master Ren Ding, from Sang Po, Henan province, Muslim. He was working in the fur business and lived on 5th road of Shanghai). Knowing that Lu was teaching in Shanghai, Master Ding watched him for many days before went to meet him. Master Lu knew Master Ding was famous and respected him very much. After checking Lu's skills, Ding said, you can carry my work now. In more than half of a year, Lu went to the Muslim temple and learned Xinyi Liu He Quan (Xinyi Six Harmony Quan) from Master Ding privately.

Mr. Lu with his whole life spent on studying, teaching, practicing and improving Chinese Martial Arts, he created his own style–Lu style Xinyi Liu He Quan（Xinyi Six Harmony Quan）which has spread since the 60's. He was the first master of Shanghai Xinyi Quan.

盧式心意大師**王書文**老師

王書文老師是現任「盧式心意拳」的會長，是盧師如今在世弟子中的長師兄。

王老師生於1919年，山東萊州人，自幼便隨著家鄉的武術老師學習武術，1936年在上海開辦了美華大理石工業社，同年跟隨「中原大俠」王效榮老師習武。後經王效榮老師引見，於1938年開始跟隨盧師學習盧式心意六合拳，經過盧師一年多的考察，1939年王老師和王佩、李儀華三人同時向盧師遞貼拜師。

王老師跟隨盧師學藝二十餘年，對待盧師就像對待自己的父母一樣。盧老師也很喜歡王老師，公園裡

練好後，經常到王老師家或帶王老師到山東會館空房間單傳獨授，說到興奮處，連比劃帶打。盧老師晚年常對王書文老師說：

「書文，你要好好努力下把勁，趁我現在還能教，等我『無償了』（河南回民方言死了的意思），我還能帶到棺材裡不成？這門拳是古上留下來的寶貝，花錢買不到的，你要堅持傳下去，不能失傳，也不能亂傳。我以後只是圖落個名。拳不複雜，但易學，難練，更難精，拳藝非常的深奧，你要去撈，越撈越深，要勤學苦練，學到老，練到老。」

盧老師去世後，王老師仍和大師兄李遵賢、師弟楊肇基一起共同研習，遍訪師兄師弟，整理拳譜。日就月將，更感它的珍貴，不敢有一絲的懈怠。

盧式心意六合拳入門

The Chairman of the Association of the Lu style
Xinyi Quan – Master Shuwen Wang

Master Wang is the Chairman of the Association of the Lu style Xinyi Quan. Within Master Lu's students who are alive, he is the most senior. He was born in 1919, Lai Zhou, Shandong province. He started to learn Martial Arts with a teacher in his hometown during his childhood. In 1936, he started up a company named the America – China Marble Industry Group in Shanghai. In the same year, he started to follow Master Xiaorong Wang (Zhong Yuan knight – errant) (Zhong Yuan area hero – knight-errant in the central areas of China). In 1938, Master Xiaorong Wang recommended him to Master Lu to learn the Lu style Xinyi

Liu He Quan(Xinyi Six Harmony Quan). After being reviewed for a year by Master Lu, he, Pei Wang, Yihua Li became Master Lu's disciples at the same time.

Being Master Lu's favorite student, Master Wang followed him for 20 years. They treated each other like father and son. Master Lu gave him many individual lessens. In Master Lu's later years, he indicated to him frequently："You must do your best to learn my techniques and skills. I do not want to take them to the tomb. These priceless treasures came from the hard work of generations and generations. You must carry it on and pass it to the next generation. Do not lose it and do not pass it to irre-sponsible people. Otherwise, my efforts would be in vain. The skills are not complicated, but it is difficult to practice and

more so to achieve perfection. The art is very profound. The harder you work, the more you know. You must be consistent in working and practicing until you are old."

After Master Lu pasted away, Master Wang with his Xinyi Quan brothers: Zhunxian Li, Zhaoji Yang, visited all the disciples of Master Lu, organized the theories and specifications. The more he worked, the more he cherished it, never slacking.

盧式心意・常識

The Elegancy of Lu Style Xinyi

Common sense

盧式心意六合拳入門

一、概　述

　　盧式心意六合拳，簡稱：盧式心意，上海人又喜歡稱之謂「十大形」，以「實用、長壽、易上手」為特色。

　　這是一門在滬形成、發展、壯大，具有上海文化內涵、精神氣質、深受滬上百姓喜愛的功夫。他成於上海、名於上海、榮於上海，是海派文化中唯一一門得到國內武術界認可，又深受國內、外功夫界人士愛戴的拳種，是大上海武文化的優秀代表。

　　他源於河南心意六合拳，是一代宗師盧嵩高武術大師對傳統武術開創性的繼承與創新。他是海派文化與黃河文明相互交融的結果，他既有海派文化的「逸」性，取法自然、和順，講究渾然天成而又得之巧、得勢又得韻、去其糟粕而得其精；然又不失黃河文化的綿厚、博大、方正之心。他取法自然，將現代融於傳統，不斷取法，不斷進步。中國人講：人品做到極時，只是本然；文章寫到好時，只是恰好；武藝練到高時，只是合順。合天、合地，合身；順勢、順時、順手，伺機而動，順勢而行，講虛實，更講明了——大道至簡——化繁為簡——化簡為至，適合大都市人的生活節奏與習慣，更適用現代城市人的不斷進取之心。

「腰腹為中節，足腿為根節」。然分而言之，則「三節」之中，亦各有「三節」也。

41

盧式心意・常識

他拳性至明，就是對生命強有力的維護，不使生命受損、人格受辱。學習盧式心意拳入手至簡，動作至明，目地至白，就像學寫中國的書法一樣，每日練習，每日都有進步。進步總是快樂的，日就月將，點橫之間，必將韻味十足，往來與起落之間蘊寓生機與人性之美。

盧式心意是一門養生拳，具有長生性。拳總的歌訣為：「靜養靈根氣養神，養功養道見天真；丹田養就千斤寶，萬兩黃金不予人。」長期練習盧式心意拳的人都具有長生性，這不是個別現象，而是普遍性高壽，如盧嵩高老師、尚學禮老師、楊殿卿老師、解興邦老師……都是高壽之人，在世的王書文老師，90高齡仍能行拳授課，心明體健。

盧式心意拳六合拳是上海寶貴的文化遺產。

1. The Summery of Lu style Xinyi Quan

"Lu Style Xinyi Liu He Quan (Six Harmony Quan)", in short "Lu Style Xinyi", is also called "Shi Da Xing" (Ten Big Postures) by people in Shanghai.

Lu Style Xinyi Quan is a one of the Martial Arts that was formed and developed in Shanghai, and flourished there. It showcases Shanghai's culture and is well-loved by the common people of Shanghai. Among the native Shanghai conventional

Wushu schools, it is the only one to be acknowledged by the national Wushu world. It has now become the symbol of Shanghai Wushu culture and is appreciated by many Wushu enthusiasts in its homeland and abroad.

Lu Style Xinyi Quan, derived from Henan Xinyi Liu He Quan (Henan Xinyi Six Harmony Quan) is a creative achievement of the great Wushu master Lu Songgao. He carried on and renovated traditional Wushu. Lu Style Xinyi Quan combines Shanghai style culture with that of the Yellow River's. It inherits the naturalness, gentleness, refinement, and vitality of the former and the openness and fairness of the latter. It is enlightened by nature and integrates modern elements into the traditional. There is a Chinese saying: "One can only have good character if that's who he is. One can only write a good article if what's written is appropriate. One can only achieve a high status in martial skill when he is at the level most compatible for himself." Comply with the heaven, the earth, and the body. Comply with power, time, and movement. Move at the right opportunities. It also tells us that the greatest theory comes from the simplest law. Turning the complicated into the simple and the simple into the practical is not only suitable for the urban tempo, but also for the enterprising spirit of the urbanite.

The goal of Lu Style Xinyi Quan is very clear: to protect one's life from harm and one's dignity from being insulted. Studying

Lu Style Xinyi Quan should start from the simplest movement. Practice it precisely and attain the goal purely. Similar to learning Chinese calligraphy, one should practice it every day, and make progress every day. Day after day, you would find lingering charm emerging and the vitality and beauty that accumulates in the strokes.

Lu Style Xinyi Quan is a health – supporting martial art and plays a role in attaining longevity. There is a saying: "Stand still to cultivate the spirit; circulate the Qi to refresh the mind; see the great truth; treasures nurtured in the body cannot even be traded for gold. It is not a coincidence that those who practice Lu Style Xinyi Quan have longer lives. The great masters, such as Songgao Lu, Xueli Shang, Dianqing Yang and Xingbang Xie, all lived long lives. Mr. Shuwen Wang, at the age of 90 years old, still maintains a good health and a clear mind. He not only continues to practice martial arts, but also teach disciples.

Lu style Xinyi Quan is a precious cultural inheritance of Shanghai.

二、解　釋

盧　式

指盧式心意拳的開山鼻祖、一代宗師盧嵩高武術
大師所開創的武術一派之功夫。

心

要有一顆必勝之心。擁有了一顆勇敢的、必勝的
心，才能做到鬥志昂揚，一如山上滾落下來的一塊頑
石，不論大小無人敢接，無人敢擋。

意

動手之意，一種本能反應，聞風而動，相機而
行。本能的選擇時機、方向、沾實一點……「能在一
思前，莫在一思後。」

六合

拳譜曰：「心與意合、意與氣合、氣與力合；膀
與胯合、肘與膝合、手與足合。」是一種保持身體協
調如一，攻與守相對合理的方法。猶如什麼八卦陣、
梅花陣……一樣，千萬人能合而為一，進可攻、退可
守，命令如一，反應迅速的方法。

拳

一為運動軌跡、技術方法；二為文化之絡，待人
之法。

2. Terminology

Lu Style Xinyi: Created by WuShu Master Lu Song Gao.

Heart: Full of confidence, courage, and high spirits; like a big stone rolling from a top of a hill, no one can come close or hold it back.

Mind: Ready to fight. Watch for a chance and take action. Move fast, faster than the thought and before the opponent can react.

Liu He (Six Harmonies): Heart and mind are unified as one; mind combines with Qi (internal energy); Qi combines with force (strength); arms and hips combine; elbows and knees are one; hands and feet are one. Co - ordinate the entire body to attack and defend in an adequate way. To create the ideal of the Eight Diagrams Matrix or Plum Flower Matrix (troops in ancient China change matrixes during fighting), thousands of people unite as one. When moving forward to attack or moving back for defense, follow the command and act fast.

Quan: There are two meanings. First, it can represent movements or techniques. Second, it can be culture related and represent manners with people.

三、成　式

這裡講的一些成式名稱與盧式心意拳動作名稱相符，但要求不同，要區別認識。

3. Techniques and Postures

The Techniques and Postures mentioned here are basic Xinyi skills and may be somewhat different from the Lu Style.

牮杆之式

身體與支撐腿一如一根大杆一樣頂於地上，勁如一貫通。

Prop Pole

One leg supports the body like a pole on the ground. The force is straight.

夾剪之式

身體坐於兩腿上，或前或後，前腿小腿**垂直**於地面，後腿大腿**垂直**於地面。

Clip and Cut

The body sits on the legs. One leg is forward, the other behind. The lower part of the front leg is perpendicular to the ground. The thigh of the back leg is perpendicular to the ground.

三尖照

鼻尖、膀尖、腳尖朝一個方向。坐意，後腳**平**可前腳**翻**，聽風而起，起如浪翻。

Three Points in Accordance：

Nose, shoulder, and toes are pointed in the same direction. Intend to sit. The foot in the back steps on the ground. Lift the toes of the front foot. Move with the sound of the wind, like a wave.

三尖齊

鼻尖、膀尖、腳尖垂直而齊。
前意，前腳平可後腳抬，聞風而
動，動如挑擔。

Three Points Aligned

Nose, shoulder, and toes are
in the same vertical line. Intend
to move forward, the front foot on
the ground, the back foot lifted.
Go into action with the sound of
the wind. Move as if carrying two
pails with a pole.

寶劍出鞘式

膀與胯合，逆勢，**逆手逆腳**。

Bao Jian Chu Qiao（Sword Out of the Scabbard）

A shoulder corresponds to the hip at the other side.

開弓放箭式

膀與胯合，順勢，**順手順腳**。
Kai Gong Fang Jian（Draw a Bow）：

A shoulder corresponds with
the hip on the same side.

虎抱頭式

以把護腮、胸，內掛外裹。

Hu Bao Tou（Tiger Embraces His Head）

Protect the cheek and chest. One hand does an inward parry and the other swings outward.

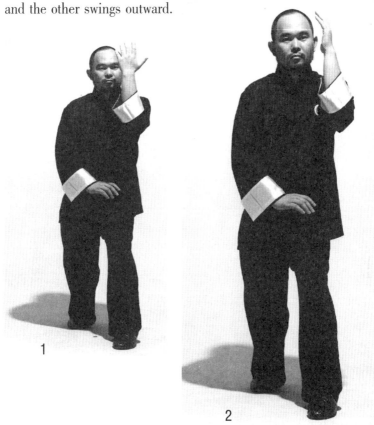

1

2

註：內掛：用大拇指側的手臂格擋。

Nei Gua（Inward Parry）: Parry with the side of the arm on the same side of the thumb.

貓洗臉式

以把護腮、胸，外掛內裏。

Mao Xi Lian（Cat Washes His Face）

Protect the cheek and chest. One hand parries outward and the other swings inward.

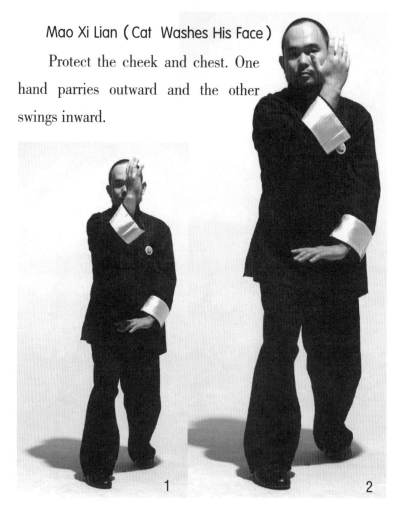

註：外掛：用小拇指側的手臂格擋。

Wai Gua（Outward Parry）：Parry with the side of the arm which is on the same side of the little finger.

拔劍式

以把護腹、襠，外掛外裹。

Ba Jina Shi（Hold the Handle of Sword）

Protect the cheek and crotch. One hand parries outward and the other swings outward.

註：外裹：手臂從人體中心線往手臂同側方旋轉。

Wai Guo（Swing Outward）：Rotate the arm form the middle
line of the body outward to the same side.

插劍式

以把護腹、襠，內掛內裹。

Cha Jian Shi（Sword Into the Scabbard）

Protect the cheek and crotch. One hand parries inward and the other swings inward.

註：內裹：手臂從人體中心線往手臂異側方旋轉。

Nei Guo（Swing Inward）：Rotate the arm from the middle line of the body outward to the other side.

龍折身式

意如豎碑，折斷中節，中之梢節不動（頭），中之根節前打（腹）。腰有轉軸之能，雙肩一陰翻一陽。

過步：後腳抬而前，落於前腳前。後腳動而前腳不動。

墊步：後腳抬而前，落於前腳後。後腳動而前腳不動。

寸步：前腳抬而前，落於前腳前。後腳不動前腳動。

疾步：後腳抬而前，落於前腳處。後腳未落前腳抬。

Long Zhe Shen （Dragon Bends）

The mind is determined like an upright stone tablet. Bend at the middle section of the body. Keep the head upright. Push the stomach forward. The waist is acting as an axle. The shoulders roll over to exchange Yin and Yang.

Guo Bu (Over Step) – The back foot steps forward before the front foot. The front foot does not move.

Dian Bu (Skip Step) – Lift the back foot and place it behind the front foot. The front foot does not move.

Cun Bu (Inch Step) – Lift the front foot and step forward. The back foot does not move.

Ji Bu (Quick Step) – Lift the back foot and place it where the front foot stands. Lift the front foot before the back foot

盧式心意六合拳入門

touches the ground.

垂肘

肘尖垂於地面，**內裹**，肘不離肋。

Chui Zhou (Sink Elbow)

Droop the elbow to the ground, swing inward, and keep it touching the ribs.

鵬肘

肘尖外**翻**起，**外掛**，肘離開肋。

Peng Zhou (Roc Elbow)

Swing the elbows outward and keep them away from the ribs.

四、把

盧式心意中的「把」不同於傳統意義武術中的掌，正是由於這一點不同，反映了心意拳的源淵和智慧。「把」有兩種解釋，一為手形；二為一組拳或一趟拳。

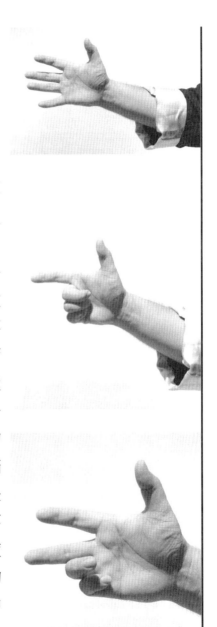

「把」（手形）——五指乍開，把心內扣，虎口要圓、要拔、要伸、要扣。相傳說心意拳是祖師爺由槍中化得的，所以握槍之手與拳中之把有諸多共通之處。精研過大槍的人都知道握槍之手不是滿把抓、滿把都用勁，而是十指各有分工，各有不同，各司其職。同樣，盧式心意拳也細化了指法的不同含義，使其在交手中占得先機。

盧式心意六合拳入門

拔拇指主中定，拔滿為升，拇指為土，管自身；拔食指定方向，千夫所指，食指為木，指敵人；拔中指主向前，以一到底，中指為火，主進攻；拔無名主左右，圓中見橫，無名為金，主防守；屈小指主後撤，以意為先，小指為水，主後退。

4. Ba

"Ba" in Lu style Xinyi is different from "palm" in the traditional WuShu, which demonstrates its origin and wisdom. "Ba" has two definitions. One is hand posture; the other is a movement or a routine.

Hand Posture – Extend the thumb and fingers. Tuck in the centre of the palm. The tiger mouth is round and stretched. It is said that Xinyi was created from a spear technique by the founder. Therefore, they have much in common. Those who are good at using the spear know not to hold it with full hands. Every finger has its own responsibility. Similarly, in Lu style Xinyi, figure movements have different meanings, which may create advantages in competition.

An extended thumb shows determination. The thumb represents earth, which is responsible for self control.

An extended forefinger shows direction. The forefinger represents wood, which is used to point to enemies.

An extended middle finger means to go forward and attack. The middle finger represents fire, which is responsible for an attack.

An extended third finger means defense. The third finger represents gold, which is responsible for defense.

A curved little finger means to draw back. The little finger represents water, which is responsible for retreat.

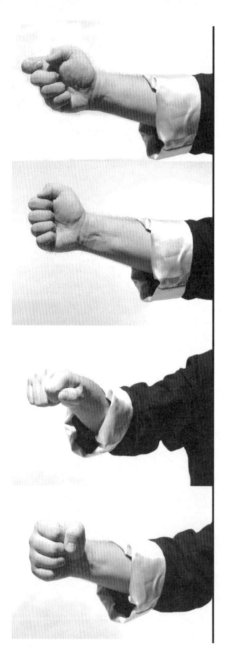

五、拳

盧式心意習慣性稱拳為錘，拳性似炮，所以多講炮錘。錘形有二：

一為五指折疊成拳，先折小指、無名指，然後疊小指、無名指，再折疊中指，食指只折不疊，大拇指壓在食指上，成其盧式心意拳獨特的門鼻拳，行拳時以食指的第二關節為鋒（門鼻拳：象形於用食指與大拇指夾著門鼻關門的手形）。

二為五指折疊成拳，先從小指開始，依次到食指，大拇指折疊壓在食指、中指的第二關節上。

　　鷹捉：由把成拳的過程就是鷹捉。出手如搓，回手是鈎。

　　三者關係：沾實的瞬間或由把變拳，或由拳變把，或由把變為鷹捉。由拳變把，我們叫丟把，如手中有物，丟棄，把心內吐。把心與肘尖，或與肩尖形成兩點一線的撐拔關係。由把變拳是沾實的瞬間向上或向前。由把變為鷹捉是沾實的瞬間向下或向後。

5. Chui

Lu style Xinyi calls a fist as a hammer："Chui". A fist strikes like a cannon. Therefore it is also called a cannon hammer ("Pao Chui"). There are two hammer (fist) postures.

First： bend the little finger, the third finger and middle finger, and then fold them. Bend the forefinger with a space between the first section and the third section. Press the thumb on to the forefinger to form a Lu style "Men Bi Fist". (Men Bi is a hook on a door that latches it shut) This means to form a hook with the thumb and the forefinger). Deliver the force to the second section of the forefinger

Second： Bend all the fingers from the little one to the forefinger and press the thumb onto the second section of the forefinger and middle finger.

大抵以中平為宜，以正直為妙，與「三節」法相合，此又不可不知也。

盧式心意六合拳入門

Ying Zhuo(Eagle Claw)

The movement that from palm to fist is called"Eagle Claw".

The relation between Ba, Quan, and Ying Zhuo

At the moment that touch target, turn the fist into an opening palm or turn the opening palm into fist, or turn the opening palm into eagle claw.Turn the fist into an opening palm, we name it "Diu Ba", like take something in hand, then throw it out. The central of the palm to line with the tip of elbow or the tip of shoulder.Turn the opening palm into fist is the force goes up and straight at the moment that touch target.Turn the opening palm into eagle claw is the force goes down and back at the moment that touch target.

六、身成六勢

（雞腿、龍腰、熊膀、鷹爪、虎豹頭、雷聲）

習盧式心意者，行每一把拳都不可不顧身成六勢。它是盧式心意拳門人日常之身法。不明身成六勢等於不懂盧式心意，身不成六勢等於不會盧式心意。

整身而言，腰以上為上半身，腰以下為下半身，上半身要穩穩地坐在下半身上，如同坐在車上、騎在馬上一樣放鬆，以腰脊為軸、為杆插在下半身上。下半身如同車的底盤一樣要承載住車的上半身。往來之間上半身要相隨下半身。

交勇對峙，上半身的狀態如同一顆迫擊炮彈下落至撞針上的一瞬間，又一如持槍之手已在半連動，蓄而未發，身勢已成，才能做到後發先至。上半身的穩、準、狠是要建立在下半身穩、實、厚的基礎上。

1. 雞 腿

腰以下的部位，含整個根節，胯前掖後翻、閉股、提襠、豎膝、屈腿、折腕，如同車的底盤、炮的底架，要將本重與所承受的重量都穩穩地落在腳下、地上。

運動過程中，要用翻胯之力，以胯拎大腿、提膝、翻腳而前。兩大腿內側、兩膝、兩腳踝骨有相合之意，磨脛而出。兩膝揉動前行，一膝頂、一膝豎，如機器人前行時的下半身狀態。身如坐轎，豎起腰脊，這樣才能保證所有重量通順地落於地上，不在胯、膝、腕部受力，否則日積月累會形成慢性膝傷。

從身體正面看，雞腿站立時，人會微微傾斜。如左勢雞腿，人會微微右前傾，此時，須盡力保持中正，保持向左方向的中正之勢。此處的關竅在於左小腿的前外側肌肉工作，身領而前、前而上，這樣身在運動過程中自無左右搖擺之醜態。否則身如左右微搖，則腳下無根，力出不順，身無中正，敗局已定。

雞腿曲折有形，沾實一點時，支腳要撐地、爭膝、開胯、完成幾個力和速度的相累加，完成身體的三翻九轉，形成整體發力，全身一體，成一動無不動之勢。

2. 龍腰

龍腰指胸腔與盆腔的之間的整個部分，中節之根節，身之縱橫都賴於此。

習盧式心意拳者，腰須練的極度靈活，將髖關節通過扭、曲、伸、拔等手法鍛鍊得非常靈活、鬆動，且有筋骨之力。龍腰，一是要練出橫勁，具體的講就是，透過日就月將的練習龍調膀，脊柱兩側後腰帶處會各自練出一塊橫向肌裡的肌肉，腰愈圓才能有橫勁愈大，這就是心意拳出手打橫不見橫的關竅。二要練出束展勁。盧師常講：「皮老虎、皮老虎，束之如貓，縱之如虎」，就是靠腰脊的彎曲，胸腔與盆腔合，透過日就月將的練習龍折身，腹部自會練出一塊塊縱向肌裡的肌肉，腹愈實束展才會勁愈足。這樣，發力時自會出全身的整勁，而手無忙亂多餘的動作，方做到手與身束一。

王書文老師常說：「手到腳不到，犯擒拿；腳到手不到，犯跌法。」欲避此病，須將龍腰練出。

3. 熊膀

胸腔上與後相連的部分，含膀與背至肘。胸腔在脊骨的撐撥下欲上，熊膀在引力的作用下欲落，一如人與穿在人身上的衣服關係，身欲上衣欲下。人體與熊膀的關係，保證了人能直立行走。習盧式心意拳要時時加強這層關係的保持，爭愈強人愈穩。胸腔不會動而熊膀在肌肉與筋的作用下，會前後上下移動，形成胸的開合、兩膀間的上下之爭，從而有了束展勁，六合形。

膀關節應透過掄、伸、拔等方法，將韌帶拉長，鍛鍊關節靈活，將勁力由筋骨傳遞。「前如瓦攏，背如鍋」，「背不圓，力不全」，力自腳下出，由腰，脊，背的加速傳遞，在發力過程中，背部，膀部的肌肉和韌帶會在發力的一瞬間鼓實收緊，這樣，一是保證勁與力在傳遞時的線性，二是減小對自己的身體的衝擊，擠壓，以免對腰脊形成慢性傷害。

內家拳講的含胸拔背，沉膀垂肘，指的是背部挺拔，脊骨如一節節挺起，背微向前校正，脊骨上下兩端相掙，胸部放鬆，脊骨正人才能正。

4. 鷹捉

鷹捉泛指肘以下的部分，小臂與把。由把成拳的過程中就是鷹捉。「回手是鉤」講的就是鷹捉的形與法。練習者手上須有筋骨之力。王書文老師講：「須練就四梢勁，甲為筋梢，甲欲透骨。」甲透骨即有鷹捉之功。常人練拳，多力在掌根、掌心、指根處滯留，故力不通透，達不到梢節。

5. 虎豹頭

指雙膀以上的部分，含頭與項。領而豎就是訣。練拳時，兩耳要聽而上領，下頜應水平後收，頭中正不歪斜，頸椎受力後自會有上頂之勢，而無上頂之形。頸部挺拔，如虎豹之勢。髮為血梢，心驚發乍而豎，有衝冠之勢。突目視人，眼有三法：觀天不看天，察地不看地，眼角灑人。前有三條路，左、中、右，心有所動，舌有所指，他人無意我在先。舌為肉梢，舌欲催齒。牙為骨梢，有勇在骨，牙欲斷筋，切齒之恨，有虎之形狼之心。

身成六勢的虎豹頭與心意拳動作中的虎抱頭有區別，練者應分開。一是身形的要求，一是動作的名稱。

6. 雷 聲

梢隨聲起，聲隨梢落，一技動百技搖。習時，力出於皮糙肉厚、伸筋撥骨，勁來自於氣炸、血蕩、五藏六腑束展。勁是沿著肌肉中肌裡線性傳遞的，皮包肉、肉載力，肉厚則力大，勁的傳遞愈疾、猛。聲起，皮緊、肉縮、筋固，氣血聚而極，五藏束而實，一如火塞在氣缸中下落；心猿一動拳始出，收極而炸，一如炸缸，氣炸、血蕩，六腑展而大，充氣血於皮，皮堅發豎；充氣血於肉，肉脹筋長；充氣血於膜，骨硬筋韌。梢落有向，勁隨而至，沿直線沾實於一點，一氣呵成。此一循環所產生的惡氣順氣道噴發而出，噴的愈疾，量愈大、勁愈短、力愈猛、穿透性愈強。氣管、聲帶隨氣壓的衝擊下，而噴吐出短暫的「噫」聲，形驚、勢乍、毛豎、如獅虎狀。

6. Six Body Postures

If one wants to learn Lu Style Xinyi, he must learn the six body postures first. These are the foundation of Lu Style's routines.

People who do not know the six postures can not understand Lu style Xinyi.

For a human's body, the part above the waist is called upper body, the part below the waist is called the lower body. The upper body is stable and relax, as if sitting in a car or riding a horse. The waist is used as an axis. The lower body must be strong to support the entire body to move forward or backward in a vertical line.

When fighting, the upper body is ready and alert like a mortar bomb touching a firing pin, or as if a hand pulling a trigger in half way, which assures that one can always be faster than the enemies. The stability and the accurate movements of the upper body rely on a strong and solid lower body

1. Ji Tui (Chicken Leg)

Chicken Leg involves the lower body, including the base of the waist and legs. With movements: twisting the hips, pushing the buttocks in, lifting the crotch, straightening the knees, bending the legs and ankle, the lower body is always like base plate under the car or a cannon to support the weight steadily. The whole weight falls on the feet to the ground.

During the movement, twist the hips to deliver the force; the hips lead the thighs. Lift the knees and feet with toes pointing up and move forward. Intend to push the thighs, knees and ankles together. Move forward, rubbing the lower leg, kneading the knees. Push one knee forward, straighten the other. Walk like a robot. The upper body as if sitting on a sedan chair. Keep the waist and spine upright. The weight goes to the ground in straight line. Otherwise, the hips, knees, and ankles may be injured by moving the wrong way day in day out.

From the front, one can see that chicken stance is leaning slightly. For example, in the Left Chicken Stance, one would lean to the right front slightly. Therefore, when you practice Chicken Leg, you should try to keep your body upright. The trick is to use the muscles of the lower leg and draw the upper body forward and upward, which would avoid swing in the movement. Otherwise, the upper body swings as if there is nothing rooting the foot to the ground; the force can not go out fluidly. If one can not keep the upper body stable and upright, he would fail for sure.

Bend the leg to a suitable position; straighten the knee; push the ground with the supporting foot; open the hip. Gather force and speed to complete the movement. Unify all the parts of the body into one. Move one part, and the others follow immediately.

2. Long Yao (Dragon Waist)

Dragon Waist is the body part between chest and pelvis. It is foundation of the upper body. All the movements depend on

盧式心意六合拳入門

it.

To learn Xinyi, one needs to train the waist to be strong and alert. Practice twisting, bending, stretching, and pulling to make it agile, relaxed, and powerful. To practice Dragon Waist, one must first practice horizontal power. In other words, after practicing day by day, muscles on the both sides of the spine will be increased. The stronger the horizontal muscles are, the more power is held. That is why the Xinyi has a hidden horizontal power. Second, stretching and contracting power. Master Lu said often： skin tiger, skin tiger, bind it as a cat, release it as a tiger. Bend the spine and stretch the chest and pelvis to release the power. Practice it day by day, and the vertical muscles will form on the stomach. The tighter the stomach binds the more power it will hold.

When exploring the force, the whole body acts as one, and the hands make no unnecessary movements. Bind the hands and the body together. Master ShuWen Wang said："If the hand moves before the foot, one will be captured. If the foot moves before the hands, one will fall. In order to avoid the problem, one must practice Dragon Waist.

3. Xiong Bang (Bear Shoulders)

Bear Shoulders：The upper part of the chest connecting the back, the shoulders, and elbows. Supported by the spine, the chest is kept upright, and the shoulders hang down, similar to the clothes on the body. The relationship between the body and the shoulders enables the human being to walk upright. When practicing Lu style Xinyi, one must pay attention and strengthen this function to keep the body steady. The chest cannot move. The shoulders are driven by the muscles and tendons to move up and down, back and forth, leading the chest to expand and contract. Energy is hence generated, and the sextuple power is formed.

The ligaments in the shoulders are stretched by swinging, extending, and pulling, which transfer the force through the tendon and bones, as well as making the joints flexible.

When practicing Lu style Xinyi, there is a saying: "The front should be concave and the back convex". Another saying goes: "If your back is not round, your force is insufficient". The force is generated at bottom of the feet and then transferred through the waist, the spine and the back quickly. In the process, the muscles and ligaments of the shoulders and the back would be swelled and strained. That ensures the force is transferred in a line and the strike to the body is decreased, avoiding chronic injury to the waist and spine.

The theory of Neijiaquan, "Draw the chest up and stretch the back; sink the shoulders and elbows", means stretching the back by heaving the bones of the spine piece by piece , and bending the back forward slightly to adjust. While the chest is relaxed, the ends of the spine are pulled against each other. A body can only be kept upright with an upright spine.

4. Ying Zhuo (Eagle Claws)

Eagle Claws are the body parts under the elbows, which are lower arms and hands. In Lu Style Xinyi, when turning an opening hand into a fist, it shows the way that an eagle grabs things. When we say: "Pull the hand backward like a hook", we talk about the posture and movement of Eagle Claws. Hands must have physique power. Master Wang said: "One should improve the power of the ends. First, fingers are the ends of the tendons, which have the power of the Eagle Claws and are able to break bones. Normal people train the base of the hand or the palm or the base of the fingers more. Therefore the force can not reach the ends.

5. Hu Buo Tou (Tiger – Leopard Head)

Tiger-Leopard Head: The body parts above the shoulders, which are the head and the neck. The key point is to keep them straight. When practicing the Quan, the ears should be up and alert. Draw the chin horizontally back slightly and keep the head upright. The cervical vertebra is to be drawn up with the power of a tiger or a leopard. Hairs represent where blood circulation ends, and bristle when startled. Gaze directly. There are three postures in which to practice the eyes：seeing the sky without looking at it；sensing the earth without seeing it；observing people with split vision. Always sense three ways in front of you：left, middle, and right. The tongue points where the mind goes. The tongue represents where muscle ends and drives the teeth. The teeth represent where bone ends and drive the tendon. Courage is in the bone, hatred on the teeth, as if there is a tiger outside and a wolf inside.

Tiger – Leopard Head in the sextuple Forms is different from that in the Xinyi Quan：The former is a requirement of the body posture, and the latter is the name of a movement.

6. Lei Sheng (Sound of Thunder)

Move with roaring, and end the roaring along with the movement. One branch moves and hundreds of them follow. In practice, the power comes from the skin, thick muscles, and the stretching bones and tendons. The energy comes from the breath exploding, the blood stirring, and the viscera binding and spreading. Energy is conveyed along the texture of the muscle. The muscles are beneath the skin and carry the energy. The thicker the muscle is, the greater the energy would be, and the more quickly and fiercely the power is transmitted. Following sound, skin is strained, muscles are contracted, and the tendon is strengthened. The Qi and blood accumulates to the maximum and the viscera contracts into solidarity like a piston falling down a steam cylinder. When launching the fist with the intent of the mind, the power should be similar to the cylinder exploding at last. The Qi expands; the blood stirs; the viscera swell. Skin is filled with Qi and blood and becomes tight. Hairs stand up. Muscles are filled with Qi and blood, and expand. Tendons grow. When the membranes are filled with Qi and blood, the bones become hard and the tendon becomes tough. The flatus produced in this cycle is expelled through the trachea. The faster the speed is, the greater the amount is. The more urgent the energy, the fiercer the force, and the stronger the power is. With deep breathing, the sound of "Yi" follows. The outward appearance is alert, the action is abrupt, and hairs are standing up, resembling a tiger.

盧式心意・動作

The Elegancy of Lu Style Xinyi Motion

一、雜　說

　　過去在上海武術圈子裡流傳有：「十年××不出門，三月心意打壞人」的一句順口溜，其實這不是講誰好、誰壞的事，而是講一個入手的問題。盧式心意是從剛正入手，拳至剛、架至正，而後至柔，架會意，再者剛柔相濟，方能做到隨意用之。

　　拳剛架正是盧式心意入門時的要求。就像火車一定要在鐵軌上跑，汽車一定要行駛在公路上一樣，學習盧式心意也要遵循它的學習方法，日就月將，才能事半功倍。學習先要從梢節的盤練、變化與應用開始，而後學習中節的盤練、變化與應用，再者是根節。

　　人分三節，梢節、中節、根節。梢之梢節是「把」或「拳」，中之梢節是「頭」，根之梢節是「足」，所以初入門者要在「把上、拳上、頭上、足上」多下工夫。

　　把或拳：把打頭落起手襠，上下左右變化忙；

　　　　　　　火機一動霹靂閃，拳如炮來龍折身。

　　頭：有用意這裡不言。言身成六式以頭為首。

　　足：足打去意不落空，消息全憑後腿蹬；

　　　　　遇人交勇無須備，去意就是過地風。

　　初入門者交勇時，切記要快、快、快，要打、打、打，能在一思前，莫在一思後……寧要不是莫要停……十形合一之後才能做到拳打一記。拳譜曰：
「出手不打臉，定是藝兒淺，遇敵不可亂動忙，他有
意咱有心。」

盧式心意建拳的理念是：攻守合一，往來之間不
可不顧六合與六式，它的每一把拳都是經過精心設
計，凝聚著血的智慧。往與來、陰與陽，以迎之
（守），以圓化之，往來之間、陰陽之時以奇進之
（攻），以直打之，所以「圓中求直」是盧式心意拳
的立拳之根本。

1. By – talk

There was saying popular in Shanghai Wushu circle："For
some Wushu, even after practicing indoors for ten years, you
still can not win, but by practicing Xinyi for only three months,
you could beat others." This does not refer to a person's good or
bad deeds. It is about how to start with Xinyi. One should start
to learn Xinyi by making the fist hard and the postures right,
and then learn to be soft and allow the postures to represent the
mind. Finally, combine the soft and hard together. Only by this
way can one maximize the use of Xinyi to his free will.

Strong and correct postures are the requirements for a beginner of Lu Style Xinyi Quan. Similar to a train that must move
on the rails and a bus which must run on the road, Xinyi also

has to follow its own way, day in day out, to achieve maximum results with half the effort. Start with practicing, changing postures and applying to the end section, then the middle section, finally the root section.

The human body is divided into three sections: end section, middle section, and root section. The end of the end section is the hands; the end of the middle section is the head; the end of the root section is the feet. A novice should exercise most on the fists, the head. and the feet.

The Verses:

Fists: One fist attacks the opponent's head, one fist guards the crotch. Move and change postures quickly. Catch the moment, hit with the speed of lightning and the power of a cannon.

Head: The leader of the Six Forms of the body.

Feet: Kick with intention and without failing. Tricks come from the back leg. No warm up, kick as the wind sweeping over the ground.

When getting into a combat, one must remember: fast, fast, fast, and strike, strike, strike. Move before, rather than after thinking; one would rather be wrong than quit. Only by unifying the Ten Forms into one can one achieve the purpose of a punch. The book says: if you can not reach an opponent's face, your Gongfu (or Kungfu) is inadequate. When facing an opponent, do not take action in haste, and always be alert and ready for an other's intention.

The main principle of Lu Style Xinyi is to unite offense and defense. The Six Harmonies and Six postures must be considered in all the movements. Every action has been designed elaborately with painstaking effort and wisdom. For defense, switch Yin and Yang to block the attack directly and move in a circle to lead the attack away. For offense, exchange Yin and Yang to strike unexpectedly and directly. The direct residing in the circular is the foundation of the Lu Style Xinyi Quan.

二、定步搖閃把

（轉把、塌把、撑把、閃把、攢把）

下式

轉把

塌把

是模仿雞在爭鬥時閃進閃出時的動作模樣。這一把拳中含有五把藝：轉把防頭，塌把護胸，撑把守襠，閃把進身，攢把打人。初以肩為圓心，畫圓而行，圓中求直，圓中套圓，圓是守，直是攻。發力的方法方式一如往紅酒杯中注酒，轉把、塌把、撑把，沿前胸貫落，閃把，沿後胸貫起，攢把，後腿蹬，貫出中節，到沾實一點。學會雙手束一，同操一勢。

下式：雙把暗合，前把小臂約垂直於地面，大臂撑拔約平行於地面，大拇指應敵；後把虎口頂扶於前把的肘尖，小臂約平行於地面。

轉把：前把由大拇指應敵，旋轉為把心應敵，以肘尖至中指尖為軸（罩意）。梢之中節

（肘）、根節（膀）不動，只動梢之梢節（把）。前把根沾實，翻轉有砸拍之意。身有前意。

塌把：雙把暗合，兩虎口暗扣，一齊豎把折腕，把與肘內折約為90°角。垂肘、沉膀下塌，把塌極而止。前把小臂約與地面平行。

把根沾實，有按埋拍砸之意。身有坐意。

擰把：前把由豎把，把心應敵旋轉為大拇指朝下，以肘尖至把根部中心為軸。後把由豎把，把心應敵旋轉不大拇指朝上，以肘尖至中指尖為軸。

前把把根沾實，有按、頂、擰之意。身有前意。

閃把：後把驚而後扯，暗折小指肘後頂，以肘尖為鋒。前把後畫弧而起，腕過臍、把過膀，止於腮旁，後把虎口頂扶於前把肘尖處。

後把肘尖沾實，有頂、砸之

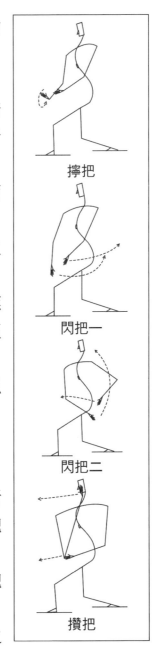

擰把

閃把一

閃把二

攢把

意。身有坐意。

攢把：前把平直而前攢，一如矢行，大拇指應敵，大臂撐拔向前以肘為鋒，大臂約平行於地面，小臂約垂直於地面；後把虎口扶於前把肘尖處催頂而前。

前把肘尖沾實，有頂、砸之意。身有前意。

2. Ding Bu Yao Shan Ba
（Standing, Swinging and Dodging）

This movement is used to imitate chickens' attack or retreat while fighting. It includes 5 skills（Holds）: Turning Hold to protect the head; Sinking Hold to protect the chest; Wresting Hold to protect the crotch; Swinging Hold to move forward; Piercing Hold to beat the enemy. At the beginning, use the shoulders as a centre of a circle and move in circles. Straight lines reside in circles; circles reside in circles. The circles are used for defense; the straight lines are used to attack. The way to deliver the force is like pouring red wine into a cup. Deliver the force downward along the front chest while practicing Turning Hold, Sinking Hold, or Wresting Hold; deliver the force upward along the back while practicing Swinging Hold; deliver the force from the middle part of the body while practicing Piercing Hold and pushing the back leg backward. Try to unify both hands as one.

Xia Shi (Low stance)

Two hands correspond. The forearm in front is almost 90° to the ground and the upper arm is parallel to the ground. The thumb is facing the enemy. The back hand touches the elbow of the front hand with the forearm almost parallel to the ground.

Zhuan Ba (Turning Hold)

The thumb of the front hand is pointing to the opponent. Turn it so that the palm is facing him. The wrist is acting as an axis. Keep the elbow and shoulder still. Move the hand only.

Deliver the force to the base of hand in front with the intention of pressing and smashing. The body is intending to lean forward.

Ta Ba (Sinking hold)

The two hands correspond, with the tiger mouths (the part between the thumb and the index finger) intending to get close. Bend the wrists to form 90° with the forearms, fingers pointing upward. Sink the elbows and the shoulders. Push down the wrists as far as possible while keeping the forearm of the hand in front parallel to the ground.

Deliver the force to the base of the hands. The body assumes a position as if intending to sit.

Ning Ba (Wresting Hold)

The fingers of the hand in front are pointing upward, the palm facing the opponent. Turn the thumb to point downward with the middle point of the elbow and wrist as an axis. The fingers of the back hand are pointing upward, the center of the hand facing the opponent. Turn the thumb to point upward with the wrist as an axis.

Deliver force to the base of the front hand with the intention to press, push and twist. The body is intending to lean forward.

Shan Ba (Swinging Hold)

Pull back the back hand as if startled. Bend the little finger swiftly and push the elbow backward. Strike with the elbow. Move the back hand in an arc, passing the navel and the shoulder, and stop beside the cheek. The tiger mouth of the back hand touches the front elbow.

Deliver the energy to the front elbow with the intention of pushing and smashing. The body assumes the tendency to sit.

Cuan Ba (Piercing Hold)

Roll the front hand forward, straight like an arrow. The thumb points to the opponent. Lead by the elbow, move the upper arm forward. The forearm is almost parallel to the ground while the upper arm is almost vertical. The tiger mouth of the back hand pushes the front elbow.

Deliver the energy to the front elbow with the intention of pushing and smashing. The body assumes the tendency to lean forward.

六曰「手足法」者：「出、領、起、截」也。

盧式心意六合拳入門

5
7
6
8

9 | 10
11 | 12

三、臥地炮（轉把、臥地把）

什麼是炮拳？像出膛的炮彈一樣打拳，拳如炮子一樣的快疾、準狠。炮彈的速度、力量來自彈殼中火藥，炮拳的速度、力量同樣來自中節氣血的貫實。臥地炮就是拳如炮子天上來，從上往下打，沾實一點時拳眼朝下，肘尖朝上。或由把變拳，或由拳變把。

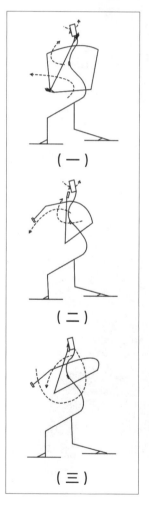

（一）

（二）

（三）

1. 開弓放箭式或寶劍出鞘式（身形）、牮杆之式或夾剪之式（腿形）、虎抱頭式或貓洗臉式（手形）都可與配合使用。

2. 寸步、過步、墊步、疾步與三角步都可（步法）。

3. 龍折身，雙膀一陰翻一陽（身法）。

4. 雙把合二為一，以拳為鋒，塌膀出勁，拳眼朝下，鵬肘，胳膊內折大於150度角，小於180度角。

5. 沾實於拳的食指與中指的拳輪，拳如炮子上邊來或平擊或下砸，三點一線的發力貫勁（膀尖：沾實一點與對手人體中軸線上的某一點）。

臥地炮（單手雙邊搖，轉把中化）

轉把：前把由大拇指應敵變化為拳眼朝裡，轉把為拳，有內掛外裹之意。

臥把：1.拳眼朝裡內旋為拳眼朝下，平擊或下砸。後把由扶於虎口處上掛，止於鼻高。

2. 身有前意。

3. 寸步。

週而復始：1. 龍折身，雙膀一陰翻一陽，以身帶拳，由拳變把。後把變前把，原前把變後把，虎口扶於前把的肘尖處，搖一閃把，止於轉把。

2. 過步。

3. Wo Di Pao (Lying Cannon)

Punch as a cannonball from the cannon, fast, accurate, and forceful. The speed of the cannonball depends on the gunpowder inside. The speed of the punch is also depends on the energy delivered. Lying Cannon is like the cannonball from the sky, punch downward, the eye of the fist facing down, the elbow pointing up. Turn the opening hand into a fist, or turn the fist into an opening palm.

1. Use Draw a Bow or Sword Out of the Scabbard as the

body posture. Use Prop Pole or Clip and Cut as the leg posture. Use Tiger Embraces His Head or Cat Washes His Face as the hand posture.

2. Step movements: Over Step, Skip Step, Inch Step, and Quick Step.

3. Dragon Bends. The shoulders roll over to exchange Yin and Yang.

4. Two hands correspond. Strike with the fist. Sink the shoulders. The eye of the fist is facing downward. Form Roc Elbows. Bend the arm inward greater than 150°, less than 180°.

5. Deliver the force to the forefinger and the middle finger. The fist goes either up, down or straight. The three points, which are the fist, the shoulder, and a point in the center of the opponent's body, are in the same line.

Wo Di Pao (Lying Cannon) – Single hand swings at both sides :

Zhuan Ba (Turning Hold) :

Turn the hand in front from its previous position (the thumb facing enemies) so that the eye of it faces upward. Turn the palm to a fist. Parry Inward. Wrap Around Outward.

Wo Ba (Lying Hold)

1. Rotate the fist inward from the eye facing inward to downward. Strike either forward or downward. Raise the back

hand to nose level.

2. The body is intending to lean forward.

3. Inch Step.

Repeat：

1. Dragon Bends. The shoulders roll over to exchange Yin and Yang. The body pushes the fist. Turn the fist to an open palm. The back hand moves forward. The front hand moves backwards. The two hands switch positions. The tiger mouth of the back hand touches the elbow of the front arm. Swinging Hold and Turning Hold.

2. Over Step.

但起前手，如鷂子鑽林，須束身翅而起。推後手，如燕子取水，

起如舉鼎，落如分磚，此雙手之法也。

四、裏邊炮（攢把、裏邊）

拳如炮，打拳像炮子出膛的瞬間一樣，驚炸之靈。拳如炮子側旁來，從斜裡打出一拳，延伸於搖閃把中的轉把，以脊骨為軸，要周正。一把用虎抱頭或貓洗臉，另一把用臂要抱圓、端平，拳眼朝上，沾實一點時中節發力。

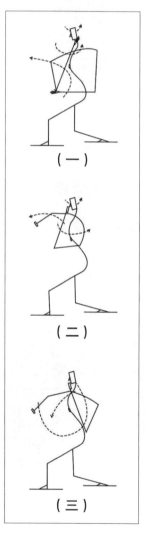

（一）

（二）

（三）

1. 開弓放箭式或寶劍出鞘式（身形）、牮杆之式或夾剪之式（腿形）、虎抱頭式、貓洗臉式、扶劍把式與劍入鞘式（手形）都可與配合使用。

2. 寸步、過步、墊步、疾步與三角步（落腳後與原來兩腳的位置成三角形）都可（步法）。

3. 龍折身，雙膀一陰翻一陽（身法）。

4. 雙把合二為一，一手裏、一手打，以拳為鋒，拳眼朝上。鵬肘，胳膊內折大於 90 度角，小於 150 度角，拳、肘、胳膊、膀在一個水平面上，以腰為軸。

5. 沾實於拳的食指與中指的拳輪，拳如炮子兩邊來，平擊，三點一線的發力貫勁（肘尖：沾實一點與對手人體中軸線上的某一點）。

裹邊炮（單手雙邊、轉把中化）

轉把：

1. 雙把合二為一，把有前後上下之分，前把大拇指應敵，手不離腮，肘不離肋，小臂約垂直於地面；後把虎口頂扶於前把的肘尖處。

2.身有前意。

3.寸步、墊步。

裹邊：

1. 龍折身，雙膀一陰翻一陽，腰有轉軸之能。

2. 以身帶把，上把裹邊可成其虎抱頭式、貓洗臉式、扶劍把式與劍入鞘式，裹而成拳。後把炮：下把外掛成拳，拳面朝下，鵬肘，拎拳上掛，拳眼朝上，拳、肘、膀在一個水平面上，以身帶把。

3. 寸步、過步、三角步

週而復始：

1. 由拳變把，雙把合而為一，把有前後上下之分，塌把，搖閃，止於攢把。

2. 過步。

其落如鷹之捉物也。「起翻落鑽，忌踢宜踩」而已。

4. Guo Bian Pao(Wrap Around Cannon)

Use fists as cannon. Punch as the moment when the cannonball leaves the cannon, scarily and suddenly. Punch like a
cannonball from the side of the body. Extend it to Turning Hold
in Standing, Swinging, and Dodging. Use the backbone as an axis
and keep the body upright. One hand is doing Tiger Embraces
His Head or Cat Washes His Face. The other arm is arched,
flat, the eye of the fist facing up, force coming from the middle
part of the body.

1. Use Draw a Bow or Sword Out of the Scabbard as the
body posture. Use Prop Pole or Clip and Cut as the leg posture.
Use Tiger Embraces His Head, Cat Washes His Face, Touch
the grip of the sword, or Sword Out of the Scabbard as the hand
posture.

2. Step movements: Over Step, Skip Step, Inch Step, Quick
Step, or Triangle Step (to form a triangle with the original position
of the feet).

3. Dragon Bends. The shoulders roll over to exchange Yin
and Yang.

4. Hands correspond. One is Wrap Around, one is parrying.
Strike with the fist. Sink the shoulders. The eye of the fist is
facing upward. Form Roc Elbows. Bend the arm inward greater

than 90°, less than 150°. The fist, elbow, arm, and shoulder are at the same level. The waist is used as an axis.

5. Deliver the force to the index finger and the middle finger. The fists come from both sides, punching straight. Three points, which are the fist, shoulder, and a point in the centre of the opponent's body, are in the same line.

Guo Bian （Wrap Around Cannon） - Single hand swings at both sides. Piercing Hold at the middle

Cuan Ba (Piercing Hold)

1. Hands correspond. One hand is at the left, the other at the right. One is above the other. Turn the thumb of the front hand to face enemies, the hand at the cheek, and the elbow by the ribs. The forearm is almost vertical. The back hand pushes the elbow of the front hand.

2. The body is intending to lean forward.

3. Inch Step, Skip Step.

Guo Bian (Wrap Around)

1. Dragon Bends. The shoulders roll over to exchange Yin and Yang. The waist is acting as an axis.

2. The body leads the palms. The upper hand swings with the postures：Tiger Embraces His Head, Cat Washes His Face, Touch the grip of the sword, or Sword Out of the Scabbard, becoming a fist. The lower palm parries and forms a fist, punching downward

with a Roc Elbow. Parry with the fist, the eye of it facing up. The fist, elbow and the shoulder are at the same level (Fling the fist in an arc or straight line). The body leads the fist.

3. Inch Step, Over Step, or Triangle Step.

Repeat:

1. Change the fists into opening palms. The two hands are corresponding. One hand is at the left, the other at the right. One is above the other. Sinking Hold, Swinging Hold and Piercing Hold.

2. Over Step.

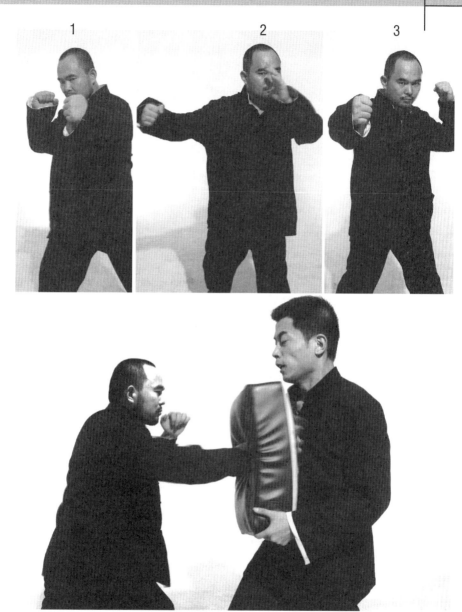

蓋腳起望膝，膝起望懷，腳打膝分而出，而其形上翻，如手之撩陰，

五、沖天炮（塌把、沖天把）

拳如炮，打拳像炮子出膛的瞬間一樣，驚炸之靈。拳如炮子地上來，由低往上打。延伸於搖閃把中的塌把，雙手塌把，整身而下，欲上先下。腳踩、身起、手上，手腳齊到，踩打合一，雙把沖天炮，拳背朝外，拳心朝裡。另一隻手依在主打手的腕下處，拳背也朝外，拳心朝裡。

塌把

沖天把一

沖天把二

　　1. 開弓放箭式或寶劍出鞘式（身形）、牮杆之式或夾剪之式（腿形）、虎抱頭式、貓洗臉式、扶劍把式與劍入鞘式（手形）都可與配合使用。

　　2. 寸步、過步、墊步、疾步與三角步都可（步法）。

　　3. 龍折身，意如豎碑。

　　4. 雙把合二為一，以拳為鋒，勁由肘部貫入，以膀為軸，合肘，胳膊內折大於90度角，小於150度角。

　　5. 沾實於拳的食指與中指

的拳輪，拳如炮子下邊來，上沖，三點一線的發力貫勁（肘尖：沾實一點與對手人體中軸線上的某一點）。

沖天炮（單手雙邊、塌把中化）

塌把：1. 雙把合二為一，豎把、折腕下塌，把有前後之分。

2. 龍折身：一頭碎碑，身有坐意。

3. 寸步或墊步。

沖天：1. 把塌到極處，前把由把變拳，以肘尖至中指拳輪為軸內旋，上沖，止於鼻高，由豎把變化為拳背朝敵、拳面朝天，以拳為鋒。後把仍豎把下按，雙把有爭意。

2. 龍折身：意如豎碑，身有沖天意。

3. 寸步或墊步，腳起而翻，腳落而踩。

週而復始：

1. 龍折身，雙膀一陰翻一陽，以身帶拳，由拳變把，由前把變後把，把有前後之分，雙把合二為一下塌，塌極而止。

2. 過步。

5. Chong Tian Pao（Punch Upward Cannon）

Use fists as cannon. Punch as the moment when the cannonball leaves the cannon, scarily and suddenly. Punch like a cannonball from the bottom of the body, Punch like a cannonball from bottom to up. Extend it to Sinking Hands in Standing, Swing and Dodging. Both hands become sinking hand, whole body rush down, if want rush upwards, rush down first. Foot stamping, body rush up, fist punch, foot and fist goes together, stamping and punching at the same time. When rush upwards, both hands turning into fists. The back of the front hand faces outward at the height of the nose. The back hand supports the wrist of the front hand.

Chong Tian Pao （Punch Upward Cannon）

1. Use Draw a Bow or Sword Out of the Scabbard as the body posture. Use Prop Pole or Clip and Cut as the leg posture. Use Tiger Embraces His Head, Cat Washes His Face, Touch the grip of the sword, or Sword Out of the Scabbard as the hand posture.

2. Step movements：Over Step, Skip Step, Inch Step, Quick Step, or Triangle Step.

3. Dragon Bends. The mind is determined like an upright stone tablet.

4. Hands correspond. Strike with the fist. Deliver the energy from the elbow to the fist. Use shoulders, each as an axis, and push the elbows together. Bend the arms inward greater than 90°, less than 150°.

5. Deliver the force to the index finger and the middle finger.

The fists come from the lower side, punching upward. Three points, which are the fist, shoulder, and a point in the centre of the opponent's body, are in the same line.

Chong Tian Pao (Punch Upward Cannon) – Single hand punches from both sides. Sinking Hold at the middle.

Ta Ba (Sinking Hold)

1. Hands correspond. Sink the wrists, fingers pointing up. One hand is before the other.

2. Long Zhe Shen (Dragon Bends) as if about to break a stone tablet with one's head. The body is intending to sit.

3. Inch Step, Skip Step.

Chong Tian (Punch Upward)

1. Sink the wrists to the maximum. Change the front hand into a fist. When punching upward, rotate the arm inward, the back of the hand facing the opponent. The back hand presses down. Push the two hands in opposite directions.

2. Long Zhe Sheng (Dragon Bends) The mind is determined like an upright stone tablet. The body is upright like a tower.

3. Inch Step or Skip Step. Raise the foot with the toes pointing up. The foot falls and stamps on the ground.

Repeat:

1. Dragon Bends. The shoulders roll over to exchange Yin and Yang. The body leads the fist. Change the fist into an opening

palm. The two hands are corresponding and exchanging positions. Sink the wrists to the maximum.

2. Over Step.

六、當頭炮（擰把、直炮）

拳如炮，打拳像炮子出膛的瞬間一樣，驚炸之靈。拳如炮子當頭來，是四炮中最快的一把拳，直來直去，一字當頭。另一把延伸於搖閃把中的擰把，或插劍式或拔劍式。

1. 開弓放箭式或寶劍出鞘式（身形）、牮杆之式或夾剪之式（腿形）、扶劍把式或劍入鞘式（手形）都可與配合使用。

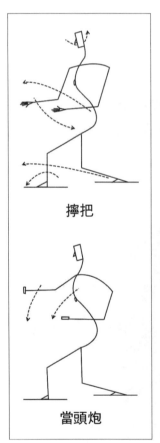

擰把

當頭炮

2. 寸步、過步、墊步、疾步與三角步都可（步法）。

3. 龍折身，雙膀一陰翻一陽（身法）。

4. 雙把合二為一，一手裹、一手打，以拳為鋒，拳眼朝上或水平，垂肘，胳膊內折大於 150 度角，小於 180 度角，拳、肘、胳膊、膀約在一個水平面上，以腰為軸。

5. 沾實於拳的食指與中指的拳輪，拳如炮子直著來，平擊或上打，三點一線的發力貫勁（膀尖：沾實一點與對手人體中軸線上的某一點）。

當頭炮（單手雙邊）

擰把：

1. 雙把合二為一，雙把塌極而止，前把前擰，有按埋之勢，後把後擰，折疊成拳，拳背朝下，拳面應敵，有爭意。

2. 身有前意。

3. 寸步、墊步。

直炮：

1. 以身帶把，前把內裹，成其劍入鞘式，後拳擰而直出，由拳背朝下翻為拳背朝上或拳眼朝上。

2. 龍折身，雙膀一陰翻一陽（身法）。

3. 寸步、過步、三角步

週而復始：

1. 龍折身，雙膀一陰翻一陽，以身帶拳，由拳變把，前把變後把，把有前後上下之分，雙把合二為一下塌，止於擰把。

2. 過步。

6. Dang Tou Pao（Straight Cannon）

Use fists as cannon, Punch as the moment when the cannonball leaves the cannon, scarily and suddenly. Punch like a cannonball at the enemy's head. It is fastest in 4 types of

Punches. Punch Straightly, directly at the head. The other hand extends to Wresting Holds in Standing, Swinging and Dodging or Insert the Sword Into the Scabbard, or Pullout the Sword from the Scabbard.

Dang Tou Pao (Straight Cannon, Wresting Hold)

1. Use Draw a Bow or Sword Out of the Scabbard as the body posture. Use Prop Pole or Clip and Cut as the leg posture. Use Tiger Embraces His Head, Cat Washes His Face, Touch the grip of the sword, or Sword Out of the Scabbard as the hand posture.

2. Step movements: Over Step, Skip Step, Inch Step, Quick Step, or Triangle Step.

3. Dragon Bends. The shoulders roll over to exchange Yin and Yang.

4. Hands correspond. One hand swings, the other strikes. Deliver the energy to the fist. The eye of the fist can be either facing upward or inward. Sink the elbow. Bend the arms inward greater than 150°, less than 180°. The fist, elbow, arm, and shoulder are at the same level. Use the waist as an axis.

5. Deliver the force to the index finger and the middle finger. The fists come from the lower side, punching straight forward or upward. Three points, which are the fist, the shoulder, and a point in the center of the opponent's body, are in the same line.

Dang Tou Pao (Straight Cannon) – Single hand punches

from both sides. Sink the wrist at the middle.

Ning Ba (Wrestling Hold)

1. Hands correspond. Sink the wrists to the maximum. The front hand twists and moves forward, intending pressing and covering. The back hand twists backward, and turns into a fist, the back of the hand facing downward.

2. The body is intending to lean forward.

3. Inch Step, Skip Step.

Dang Tou Pao (Punch Upward)

1. The body leads the hands. The front hand moves back and wrapping around inward to do Sword Into the Scabbard. The back hand twists and punches forward. Turn the hand, which is currently facing downward to face up, or the eye of the fist faces up.

2. Dragon Bends. The shoulders roll over to exchange Yin and Yang.

3. Inch Step or Skip Step, Triangle Step.

Repeat:

1. Dragon Bends. The shoulders roll over to exchange Yin and Yang. The body leads the fist. Change the fist into an opening palm. The two hands are corresponding and exchanging positions. Sink the wrists. Stop when Wresting Hold is finished.

2. Over Step.

盧式心意六合拳入門

七、熊出洞（熊舔把、熊出洞）

學習模仿熊在出洞臨敵時的動作模樣，大模大樣、入微、且少為人知。學會一個相對正確站立在敵人面前的姿勢。下式有好幾把，熊出洞是最常用的下式，盤時熊出洞，用時輕步站，熊出洞是輕步站的基礎，否則輕步站無意。輕步站意要藏得更深、形要藏得更真。

熊舔把：開弓放箭式，牮杆之式，三尖照。雙把合二為一，把有前後之分，同時出把，前把（左把）翻而上抬，把心朝上，端而上，把動而肘不動，肘不離脅，豎把而止，中指朝上，把心朝裡，把與頭合，有舔掌之意；後把按而下壓，折腕，把心朝下，止於襠上，食指罩敵。

身有前意，頂而上，有觀天不看天之形，有蔑而視之之意——眼前無人。

熊出洞：雙把合二為一，同時出把，用意不用力，前把內塌而落，鵬肘，過心過臍，止於襠

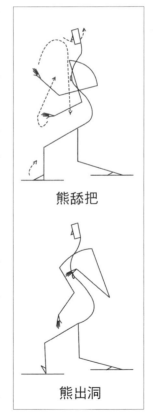

熊舔把

熊出洞

前，屈肘（大於150度角，小於180度角），中指朝下，把刃或背朝敵；後把上抬，止於乳下，腕護心，肘護脇，五指垂而下。

牮杆或夾剪之式，三尖照，含胸拔背，沉膀垂肘，身有下意，把隨身落，有察地不看地之形，盯而吃之之意——虎之恨意（熊出洞坐意已成）。

牮杆或夾剪之式，身落實而止，舔胸而前，把隨身動，翻而大拇指朝前，小指或無名指垂直於地面，一如手中有槍在。三尖齊，身有前意，有聞風而動之意（熊出洞前意）。

7. Xiong Chu Dong（Bear Exits its Den）

Imitate a bear exiting its den to face the enemy, pretentiously, subtly, but hardly noticed. Train to stand up in a right posture in front of enemies.

There are several movements of Low Stance. Bear Exits its Den is the most popular one. When you practice it, it is called Bear Exits its Den. When you use it, it is called the Light Step. Bear Exits its Den is the foundation of the Light Step. In the Light Step, the mind and intention are concealed. There are two ways to practice the bear postures: Bear Licks its Paw and Bear Exits its Den, which includes the tendency to sit and the tendency to lean forward.

Xiong Tian Ba (Bear Licks its Paw)

The postures： Draw a Bow, Prop Pole, or Three Points in Accordance. The two hands correspond, one before the other. Move the hands at the same time. The front hand (the left hand) turns and lifts up, palm facing up. Keep the elbow by the ribs unmoved；raise the hand until the fingertips point up and the palm is facing inward. The hand is at the same level of the head, as if about to be licked. The back hand bends at the wrist, presses down and stops by the crotch, the palm facing down and the index finger pointing at the opponent.

Stretch the body upward with the tendency of leaning forward. See the sky without looking at it. Scorn the enemies.

Xiong Chu Dong (Bear Exits its Den)

The two hands correspond and move at the same time, mind focused without force. Sink the front wrist and form a Roc Elbow. The front hand falls down, passing against the heart and navel and stops before the crotch. Bend the elbow greater than 150° but less than 180°, the middle finger pointing down and the side or back of the hand facing the opponent. The back hand lifts up and stops under the breast, the wrist protecting the heart, the elbow by the ribs, and the fingers hanging down.

The postures： Clip and Cut or Prop Pole, or Three Points in Accordance. Draw in the chest and stretch the back. Sink the shoulders and elbows. The body assumes the tendency to be lower and the hands follow. Observe the surroundings without looking around. Focus on the target and be ready to attack like a tiger. (This is Bear Exists its Den with the tendency of sitting)

Stabilize the body with the postures of Draw a Bow or Prop Pole. Stretch the chest and move forward. The hands follow the body. Turn the hand over, the thumb pointing forward, the little finger or third finger perpendicular to the ground, as if holding a gun. With the posture of Three Points Aligned, the body assumes the tendency of leaning forward, alert, ready to react even to the sound of the wind. (This is Bear Exists its Den with the tendency of leaning forward)

5 6
7 8

八、鷹捉虎撲把

（反背把、鵬意、鷹捉把、虎撲把）

收式有好幾把，鷹捉虎撲把是最常用的一把。盧式心意拳講：式式不離虎撲，把把不離鷹捉。是講把的往來，出手如磋，回手如鉤，在這把拳中最為體現，所以，每一把拳結束時，都要用鷹捉虎撲把收式，溫故知新，鷹捉時發雷聲「噫」，吐盡胸中惡氣，以聲驚靈。

反背把（一）

反背把（二）

反背把（三）

剪刀把：寶劍出鞘式、三尖照、夾剪之式。

龍折身：雙膀一陰翻一陽。

把隨膀走，三尖照，膀有前後之分，雙把合二為一，同時出把，中指貫勁，方能一插到底。前把後插，一如插劍入鞘，後把前插，插極而止，食指罩敵。兩肘尖相疊印於臍上。雙把以肘為軸成形似剪刀。

含胸 —— 前如瓦攏，拔背 —— 背如鍋。

軟開者，如後六勢之軟勁是也。左開用裡括，右開用外括。

　　反背把（虎擺尾）：開弓放箭式、垈杆之式。

　　前腳腳掌發力 —— 蹬，以後腳跟至頭頂為軸 —— 轉身，身體做180度的轉動，前腳變後腳。龍折身：雙膀一陰翻一陽，雙膀隨身而轉大於180度、小於270度。

　　膀隨身走、把隨膀走，雙把合二為一，同時出把，右把以右膀為圓心，以中指尖為半徑，向右後上方擺去，大於180度、小於270度。左把下塌，有按埋之意，置於右把肘下或襠上，雙把有爭意。

　　開胸發力，沾實於把背，有甩打、格擋之意，迎擊背後來襲。

　　塌把：開弓放箭式、夾剪或垈杆之式、三尖照或三尖齊。

　　身有坐意，沉而下。雙把合二為一下塌，沉膀垂肘，兩虎口暗扣下壓，塌極而止，前把小臂約與地面平行。

　　沾實把根，有按埋、拍砸、分開之意。

　　鵬意：垈杆之式。前腳跟與後腳跟合，雙腳腳跟碰而起，腳尖撐地，或起而騰空，腳五指出勁。

　　身隨腳起，身有上衝之形，有沖天之意，人微前傾。

　　把隨身起，以把領身。雙把塌極而合、合而捧，雙把把刃合而為一，大臂垂直於地面，小臂平行於地而，把背朝下。雙把捧而上，上而衝，由把成拳，大臂平行於地面，小臂垂直於地面，以拳帶身。拳的上下主次之分，右拳上，左拳置於右拳腕處，拳背朝敵，拳止於鼻高，沾實於拳面。

鷹捉（一）

衝極而落，右腳落而實，左腳出前，寸步。

身同腳落，落而成形，龍折身、寶劍出鞘式、三尖照，身有前意，有前捉之意。

把隨身落，落時錘肘於脇；由拳變把；雙把合二為一，外頂外裹，把有前後、上下之分，右把前而上，左把下而後，前把止於鼻高，左把扶於右把腕處，突目，用眼角灑人，眼光要從前把的虎口處透出。

鷹捉（二）

恨天無把：開弓放箭式、苹杆之式、、三尖照。

身有落意，身沉尾垂，龍折身：一頭碎碑——頭不動，胯往後移，翻而上，成其形，用其意。含胸拔背。寸步或寸步加墊步。

雙把合二為一，右把捉而下，左把扶上下壓，至腹前時右把後抽，有屈斷之意；左把下按，有按埋之意。

虎撲把：開弓放箭式、苹杆之式、三尖照。

雙把合二為一，以兩把食指為軸外翻，前磋，前把與前腳齊，置於膝上，後把置於襠上，把心朝下。

身有前意，垂意。意如豎碑。

寸步或原地不動完成動作。

回到站立。前腳後移或找到腳前移。

8. Ying Zhuo Hu Pu Ba（Closing）
（Eagle Grabbing and Tiger Pouncing）

There are a few movements in the closing movement. Eagle Grabbing and Tiger Pouncing are the most useful. Lu Style Xinyi says: Move forward forcefully like a tiger; pull the hand backward sharply like an eagle's claw. When a routine is closing, use the Eagle Grabbing and Tiger Pouncing to review the technique; make "Yi" sound with the Eagle Grabbing; the flatus is expelled; the sound startling souls.

Jian Dao Ba (Scissors Hold) Sword Out of the Scabbard, Three Points in Accordance or Clip and Cut

Long Zhe Shen (Dragon Bends) The shoulders roll over to exchange Yin and Yang.

The hands follow the shoulders, Three Points in accordance. One shoulder is before the other. The two hands correspond and move at the same time. Deliver the energy to the middle fingers in order to move forcefully. The front hand thrusts backward, as if inserting a sword into a scabbard. The back hand thrusts forward to the maximum. The index finger is pointing to the enemy. Both elbows overlap on the navel to form the shape of scissors,

盧式心意・動作

with the elbows as the axis.

Tuck the chest in —— the front should be concave and the back convex.

Fan Bei Ba (Turn Over) (Tiger Swing its Tail). Draw a Bow. Prop Pole.

The ball of the front foot pushes against the ground. With the line from the heel and the top of the head as an axis, turn the body 180°.The previous front foot now is at back. Dragon Bends: The shoulders roll over to exchange Yin and Yang. Shoulders follow the body to turn greater than 180° less than 270°. Shoulders follow the body; hands follow the shoulders. Two hands correspond and move at the same time. Swing the right arm upward and backward greater than 180° but less than 270°, using the shoulder as an axis. Sink the left wrist with the intention of pressing, under the right elbow or by the crotch. Push the hands in opposite directions.

Open the chest. Deliver the force the back with intention of striking and parrying backward.

Ta Ba (Sinking Hold): Use posture: Draw a Bow. Prop Pole, Three Points in Accordance, Three Points in Aligned.

Lower the body, intending to sit. Two hands correspond and sink. Sink the shoulder and elbows. With the tiger mouths (the part between the thumb and the index finger) intending to

截心者，彼眉喜面笑，言甘貌恭，而我察其有心，而迎機以截之也。

盧式心意六合拳入門

get close, push down the wrists as far as possible until the forearm of the hand in front almost parallel to the ground.

Deliver the energy to the bases of the hands with the intention of pressing, smashing, and separating.

Peng Yi (Roc Mind)：Use posture：Prop Pole. Put both heels are together. Lift the heels, Toes on the ground, or one foot off the ground. Deliver the force to the toes.

The body follows the foot, and up bursts. Lean forward slightly.

The hands follow the body; the hands lead the body. Sink the hands and hold together to unity to one. The upper arms are perpendicular to the ground while the forearms are parallel to the ground. The backs of the hands are facing down. Hold the two hands together and push up. Change the hands into fists. The upper arms are parallel to the ground while the forearms are perpendicular to the ground. The fists lead the body. The right fist is primary and is above the left hand. The left fist is beside the right wrist. The backs of both hands are facing the enemy, at nose level.

Deliver the force to the fists.

Ying Zhuo (Eagle Grabbing) (1)：Push the body upward to the maximum. The right foot stamps on the ground. Move the left foot forward with an Inch Step.

彼雖欲走而不能矣，何患其有雜計邪術乎。

盧式心意六合拳入門

5 6
7 8

9

9

10

11 12
13 14

盧式心意六合拳入門

15 16

17

九、溜雞腿（剪刀把、撕把、溜把）

模仿雞在行進時的動作模樣，悄無聲息而又疾如風。運動過程中，要用翻胯之力，以胯拎大腿、提膝、翻腳而前。兩大腿內側、兩膝、兩腳踝骨有相合之意，磨脛而出。

開弓放箭式、夾剪之式、三尖照。雙把合二為一，鵬肘，兩小臂約垂直於地面，五指乍開，三心要圓，一如農人挑擔之像。

剪刀把：寶劍出鞘式、夾剪之式、三尖照，寸步。

三尖照，膀有前後之分，雙把合二為一，中指貫勁，方能一插到底，同時出把。前把後插，一如插劍入鞘，後把前插，插極而止，食指罩敵。兩肘尖相疊印於臍上。雙把以肘為軸成形似剪刀。

撕把：開弓放箭式，夾剪之式，三尖齊。過步。

雙把插極而止，雙把對撕而

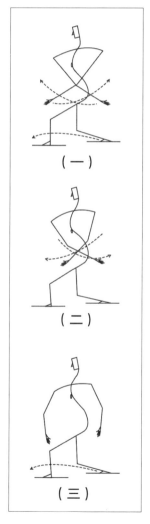

（一）

（二）

（三）

分，一如撕布。以肘為鋒，開胸出勁，沾實於把刃，雙把肘尖對稱外頂，肘尖至中指約垂直於地面，大拇指朝裡，三圓要圓。

溜把：身體的上半身不動，只動下半身，過步而前。雞腿有二，一為溜雞腿，二為踩雞步。溜雞腿貴在一個「溜」字，要以胯拎腿，頂膝出腳，腳出要翻（見身成六式之雞腿）。三要步順滑。身要平穩，無起伏。

生時慢些用力出腳，純熟時用勁出腳，如風之過草。

溜雞腿另一個盤演方法就是中平執槍，身成六式，目視前方，挺胸實腹，三尖照，前把端槍，後把壓槍於胯旁，夾剪之式，磨脛而出，身無高低起伏之形，槍頂而前行，勇者無畏。

9. Liu Ji Tui (Slipping Chicken Legs)

This movement is used to imitate chickens' marching forward, quiet and fast like a strong wind. While marching forward, use the force from the turning of the hip; use the hip to pull the leg and lift the knee; turn the foot and move forward. The inside of the legs, both knees, and both ankles are corresponding. The lower part of one leg rubs the other leg's lower part.

Chicken Slip

The postures used here are: Draw a Bow, Clip and Cut,

and Three Points in Accordance. The two hands correspond. Swing the elbows outward and keep them away from the ribs (Roc Elbow). The two forearms are about perpendicular to the ground. The fingers separate. San Xin (the center of the hands, feet, and the top of the head) are round. Move as if carrying two pails with a pole.

Jian Dao Ba (Scissors Hold)

The postures: Sword Out of the Scabbard, Clip and Cut, Three Points in Accordance, and Inch Step. At the posture of Three Points in Accordance, one shoulder is before the body, the other behind. The two hands correspond. Deliver the energy to the middle fingers in order to move forcefully. Move both hands at the same time. The front hand thrusts backward as if putting the sword into the scabbard. The back hand thrusts forward as far as possible, the index finger pointing to the opponent. Both elbows overlap on the navel to form the shape of scissors, with the elbows as the axis.

Si Ba (Tearing)

Include the postures: Draw a Bow, Clip and Cut, Three Points Aligned, and Over Step. Thrust with both hands to the maximum, and then split them as if tearing a cloth apart. With the elbows leading, stretch the chest and deliver force to the hands. Push the elbows outward in opposite directions. The forearms are perpendicular to the ground with the thumb turned inward. San Yuan (the back of the hand, the palm of the hand, and the tiger mouth) are round.

Liu Ba (Slipping)

Keep the upper body unchanged. Move the lower body forward with an Over Step. There are two techniques of Ji Tui (Chicken Leg): Chicken Slip and Chicken Step. Chicken Slip: the main point is "Slip" which is: lifting the hip, pushing the knee forward and stepping forward with the toes up (see the Chicken Leg in Six Body Postures). The steps should be smooth. Keep the upper body stable without up and down.

At the beginning, push the foot forward. When skilled, move the foot forcefully, like wind blowing over grasslands.

Another method to practice Chicken Slip: Hold a gun flat with the Six Body Postures. Eyes look ahead; stretch the chest; strengthen the abdomen, Three Points in Accordance. The front hand supports the gun; the back hand presses it by the hip. Use the posture of Clip and Cut. Move one leg forward by rubbing the shank of another leg. Keep the upper body from moving vertically. Step forward with the gun pointing ahead, full of courage.

1 2
3 4

盧式心意六合拳入門

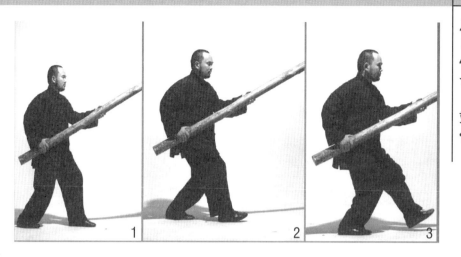

蓋志氣之帥也，氣體之充也。心動而氣即隨之，氣動而力即赴之，此
必至之理也。

十、寒雞尋食（尋食把、頂膝把）

　　學習模仿寒苦之地雞尋食時的動作模樣，一腿著
地，一腿藏暖，輪而前行。重心的轉換是雞腿行進時
在揉膝的過程中完成，後腿豎膝沉胯，前膝自頂，擠
身而進，重心移在前腿。後腳翻、後腿拎，提膝而
前，過步後腿變前腿。

尋食把

頂膝把

　　前腿一要等掛，要占好位，
從容面對；二要尋腳，腳去不空
回，見空不上，見空不打；三要
問路，尋找落腳的地方。

　　尋食把：開弓放箭式、夾剪
之式、三尖照、垂肘、寸步。雙
把合二為一，有前後上下之分，
同時搓而向前，前而尋食，折
腕，把心朝外，兩虎口暗合，後
把催前把。

　　頂膝把：寶劍出鞘式、過
步。雙把尋食而塌，過步提膝上
頂，用膝找肘，膝與肘合，肘在
外而膝在內。

　　身有前意、上意，一腿撐而
脹，一腿頂而前。

膝頂極而落，身隨膝落，把隨身落，雙把落而塌（塌把）。

週而復始：龍折身：雙膀一陰翻一陽。把隨身變，回到尋食把式。

寒雞尋食另一盤法，適宜於兩把還不能合二為一者，就是兩把抓一短棍，按：下式 —— 尋食把 —— 頂膝把 —— 週而復始。短棍的長度是中指尖至肘尖的長度，漲把為宜。

10. Han Ji Xun Shi（Chicken Seeking Food in the Cold）

Imitate a chicken seeking food in a cold field, one foot on the ground, one foot hiding in to keep warm, and walk alternately. Switch the weight while walking and twisting the knees. Straighten the back leg and sink the hip. Push the front knee up, and push the body forward, then switch the weight onto the front leg. Turn the bottom of the back foot up, and lift the leg and knee, and then take a step forward.

The front leg, first, suspends to a good position, deliberating. Second, it seeks a goal; it will not step on without goals. Third, it seeks a right place to put the foot down.

Xun Shi Ba（Seeking Food）

The postures: Sword Out of the Scabbard, Clip and Cut, Three Points in Accordance, sink the elbow and Inch Step. The two hands correspond. One hand is before the other and one is above the other. Push the hands forward in turn. Sink the wrists, the palms facing outward, the tiger mouth corresponding. The back hand replaces the front hand.

Ding Xi Ba (Push the Knee Up)

The postures: Sword Out of the Scabbard, and Over Step. Sink the wrist in a Seeking Food movement. Over Step and raise the knee to push up to meet the elbow. The elbow is outside of the knee.

The body is intending to lean forward and is kept straight. One leg supports the body, one leg pushes up to the maximum and steps forward. The body follows the knee, the hand follows the body. Sinking Hold.

Repeat:

Dragon Bends. The shoulders roll over to exchange Yin and Yang. Hands follow the body to go back the Seeking Food posture.

There is another way to practice Chicken Seeking Food in the Cold, which is suitable for a person who can not make two hands correspond. That is to hold a rod and push it down. Repeat the movement: lower the body-Seeking Food—Push Knee Up. The length of the rod equals that from the elbow to the tip of the middle finger. The rod should be thick enough to make the palms full.

1 2
3 4

抖勁崩勁太促，而難展招。

1

2

3

1　2
3　4

十一、搖閃把（溜把、踩把）

又名踩雞步，是模仿雞在爭鬥中踩打時的動作模樣，不同的是雞的踩打是在空中完成，人是在落實的過程中完成。

雞有欺鬥之勇，兩軍對壘勇者勝。

搖閃把是對上半身的要求，踩雞步講的是下半身，搖閃把在定步時多有要求。踩雞步貴在一個「踩」字。在盧式心意拳中勁有五型：「踩、撲、裹、束、絕」，雞腿有：「溜與踩」二勁，溜時用力，踩時用勁；腳出要翻，折腕翻腳，落時腳跟先著地，而後前掌，再者五指。踩，一踩二不踩，只能踩一下，寧要不是莫要停，如踩毒物，踩死不放鬆，豎膝貫勁，全身的重量落於此。

初學時，單盤時先不要用力用勁，先要保證拳架的工整，動

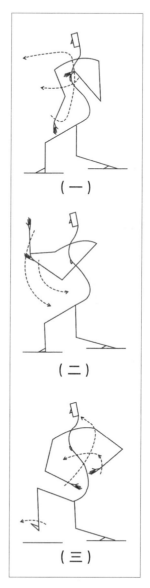

（一）

（二）

（三）

盧式心意六合拳入門

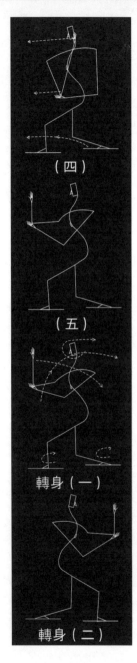

（四）

（五）

轉身（一）

轉身（二）

作的和順，手腳齊到之後再嘗試著發勁。拳譜曰：「站如鑽，走如痀。」站如鑽——形象說牮杆之式的身形。走如痀——多形容用勁踩時的身形。

單盤時先要在一較長的場地練功，純熟之後臥牛之地即可，三步一調頭，練靈活。

搖閃把（單邊搖）

溜把：身成六式、開弓放箭式、三尖照、夾剪之式，手不離腮，肘不離脅。

熊出洞下式，雙把合二為一，同時出把，前把（左）把心朝裡，貼身而上，止於鼻高，轉把，大拇指應敵，把在口出，向前；後把扶於前把虎口處前催，成形於轉把。

雙把畫圓而行，圓之中有轉把、塌把、擰把、閃把，始於轉把，止於閃把，停於腮旁，後把扶前把虎口處，畜而待出。

身有坐意，沉而前。

過步——溜雞步。

踩把：身成六式、開弓放箭式、三尖照、夾剪之式，手不離腮，肘不離脇。

雙把合二為一，沿直前攢而出，如矢之射，成其攢把。身也要攢而出。

過步——後腳翻而，出而攢、落而踩。

週而復始：溜把、踩把，圓中求直。

轉身：1.前腳腳掌發力——蹬，以腳跟至頭頂為軸——轉身，身體做180度的轉動，前腳變後腳，身有坐意，沉而下。

2.雙把合二為一，肘不動、把動。原前把變化為後把，原上把下塌，把心朝下，虎口扶於原後把肘尖處，外在；原後把上翻，在裡；胸前交叉換位。

3.轉身有格擋之意，迎後。

11. Yao Shan Ba

Imitate a chicken fighting with feet. The difference is when chickens fight with their feet, they fight in the air; but people have to fight on the ground.

Chickens are brave. When fighting with enemies face to face, people who are brave always win.

When we say Swinging and Dodging, we are talking about upper body movement. When we say Chicken Step, it is about the lower body movement. A very important point in the Chicken Step is stamping. It is one of the five strikes in Lu Style Xinyi, which are Stamping, Pouncing, Wrapping, Binding, and Cutting off. There two ways to practice Chicken Step： Slipping and Stamping. Slip with strength, stamp forcefully. Move the foot with toes pointing up, bending the ankle. When Stamping, the heel touching the ground first, then the ball of the foot, and finally the toes. Stamp forcefully, without hesitation. The force comes from the knee, and the weight of the entire body falls onto it.

For a beginner, do not use much force. Pay more attention to coordinating the whole body and moving smoothly. After the feet and hands are coordinated, then use force intentionally.

Xinyi book says： stand like a pole, walk like a lame. At the beginning, you need a bigger place to practice. When skilled, use a place as small as a lying cow to practice moving and turning flexibly.

Yao Shan Ba (Swinging and Dodging) (Single Side)

Liu Ba (Slipping)

Six Body Postures. Use Draw a Bow, Three Points in Accordance or Clip and Cut. The hand is at the cheek, and the elbow by the ribs.

Low Stance of Bear Exits its Den. Two hands correspond and move at the same time. The palm of the front hand (left hand) is facing inward, moving upward, and stopping at nose level. Then turn it to the thumb facing the enemies and move it forward. The back hand supports the Tiger Mouth of the front hand to form a Turning Hold.

Both hands move in a circle from Turning Hold, Sinking Hold, Wresting Hold to Swinging Hold. The front hand stops beside the cheek. The back hand supports the Tiger Mouth of the front hand, ready to push forward.

Lower the body and lean forward slightly with intention of sitting.

Over Step. Chicken Slipping.

Cai Ba (Stamping)

Six Body Postures. Use Draw a Bow, Three Points in Accordance or Clip and Cut. Hand is at the cheek, and the elbow by the ribs. The two hands correspond. One hand pushes forward and spins, like an arrow. Body follows the hand Piercing Hold and pushes forward.

Over Step, Lift the back foot, toes pointing up, pushing forward, and stamping on the ground.

Repeat: Slipping, Stamping, moving in a circle, strike straight.

1. Turning over: The front foot pushes the ground with its ball of the foot. Using the line from the heel and the top of the head as an axis, turn the body 180°. The previous front foot

now is at back. Lower the body, intending to sit.

2. The two hands correspond. Keep the elbow unchanged, move hands only. The original front hand now becomes the back hand. The original upper hand pushes down, palm facing down, the Tiger Mouth touching the outside of the elbow of the front hand. The original back hand pushes up and inwards. The two hands form "X" and change positions in front of the chest.

3. Turn around the body with the intention of parrying backward.

1　2
3　4

5　6
7　8

9

得和平之理，會和平之情，以和始，以和終。

10

11

不動如山岳、難知如陰陽、無窮如天地、浩渺如四海、眩耀如三光。

12　13

14　15

轉　身

十二、龍調膀（調膀把）

龍調膀：「慢若郎當龍調膀」，不緊不慢，雙膀一陰翻一陽，隨時隨地有調頭換向之意。在臆想龍的身上尋找含意與抖擻意，龍蛇纏身，一如懷中抱嬰，緊不得，鬆不得；又一如口中含玉，咬不得，不得。龍行一波三折，一如風中曬衣，有掛、有抖、有擻；又一如鐵絲穿銅錢，有拎、有上下、有晃蕩。

下式：熊出洞，雙把合二為一，兩肘鵬肘、對爭、外頂，前把肘尖至中指尖約垂直於地面，大拇指朝裡；後把下塌後拉，肘內折約150度左右，大拇指扶於膀上（打針處）。把隨肘意，對爭外頂。

調膀把：腰有轉軸之能，以腰帶膀，龍折身：雙膀一陰翻一陽，以膀帶把，把隨腰動，前把以肘尖至中指尖為軸外掛內裏，原前把變後把；後把以肘尖至中指尖為軸內掛外裏，原後把變前把。

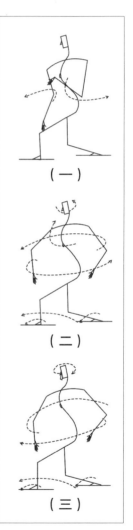

（一）

（二）

（三）

身有坐意，沉而下。

墊步──寸步──過步。三步一把，微有踏意（暗合一波三折，有水之浪意）。

轉身：前腳腳掌發力蹬，以腳跟至頭頂為軸轉身，身體做180度的轉動，前腳變後腳，身有坐意，沉而下。膀不動，把不動，前膀變後膀。

轉身有格擋之形，迎後之意。

週而復始。

12. Long Diao Bang（Dragon Adjust its Shoulders ）

The shoulders roll over to exchange Yin and Yang, ready to change directions at any time. Seek the spirit from an imaginary dragon, as if there is a snake or dragon coiling around the body, and also as if embracing a baby, one cannot be too tight, or too loose. And, as if there is a jade in the mouth, one can not bite or swallow. A dragon moves like a tide, as if to dry clothes in the wind, drifting, shivering, and arousing, and as if copper coins on a iron thread, can be picked up, put down, and swayed.

Lower body postures：Bear Exits its Den. Two hands correspond. Both elbows are Roc Elbow and push them outward in opposite directions. The forearm of the front hand is vertical to the ground, the thumb pointing inward. The back hand pushed downward and backward, the elbow bending inward about 150°, the thumb by the hip (The area normally is used for injection). The hands follow the elbows and push outward in opposite directions.

Diao Bang Ba (Adjust Shoulders) the waist is used as an axis. The waist leads the shoulders. Dragon Bends. The shoulders roll over to exchange Yin and Yang. The shoulders lead the hands. The hands follow the waist. The front hand Parry Outward and Wrap Around Outward, and then moves backward. The back hand Parry Inward and swings outward, moves forward.

Lower the body intending to sit.

Skip Step– Inch Step–Over Step. Move 3 steps forward co-ordinating with hands moving like a tide.

Turning the body over

The front foot pushes the ground with its ball if the foot. With the line from the heel and the top of the head as an axis, turn the body 180°, with the intention of dodging and parrying. The previous front foot now is at back. Lower the body, intending to sit. Keep the shoulders and hands unchanged. The previous shoulder now is at the back.

Repeat above movements.

1 2
3 4

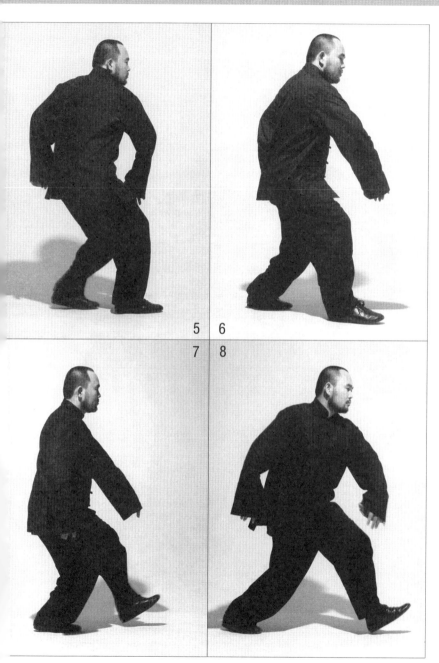

5　6
7　8

9

十三、韌性（剪刀把、撕把）

是模仿雞在爭鬥的過程中追打對手時的動作模樣。敵退我進，他敢讓，就敢追，所以這一把拳又名：追風趕月不放鬆。貴在一個字：要快、快、快……連續不斷的快、快、快……打倒他還嫌慢，望眉撩陰的名稱是用法的形像說。

剪刀把：寶劍出鞘式、夾剪之式、三尖照。

熊出洞：身有坐意，沉而下。

龍折身：雙膀一陰翻一陽，以腰帶膀。含胸拔背。

把隨身膀走，前膀變後膀，後膀變前膀。雙把合二為一，中指貫勁，方能一插到底，同時出把。前把後插，一如插劍入鞘，後把前插，插極而止，食指罩敵。兩肘尖相疊印於臍上。雙把以肘為軸成形似剪刀。寸步。

撕把：開弓放箭式、牮杆之式、三尖齊。

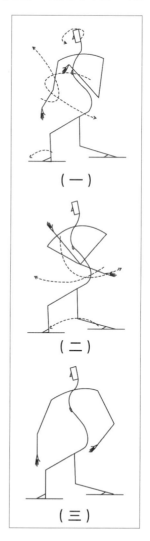

（一）

（二）

（三）

開胸出把，以兩肘為鋒，鵬肘、對爭、外頂；兩把在腹前撕而分、分而開、開而出，前把肘尖至中指尖約垂直於地面，大拇指朝裡；後把下塌後拉，肘內折約150度左右，大拇指扶於胯上（打針處）。把隨肘意，對爭外打，前把把打，後把肘頂。

身要向前，有坐意、沉而下。

過步 —— 疾步。二步一把，一氣呵成。

週而復始：剪刀把 —— 撕把。

轉身：前腳腳掌發力一蹬，以腳跟至頭頂為軸一轉身，身體做180度的轉動，前腳變後腳，身有坐意，沉而下。膀不動，把不動，前膀變後膀。

轉身有格擋之形，迎後之意。

13. Ren Jin（Tenacity）

Imitate a chicken chasing the enemies. Go forward, when the enemy retreats. Chase him, when he escapes. Therefore, it is also called Relentlessly Chasing the Wind and the Moon. A very important point is to be fast, fast, fast, though never fast enough to beat the enemy down. Beat eyebrow and crotch at the same time.

Jian Dao Ba（Scissors Hold）

Use Sword Out of the Scabbard or Clip and Cut or Three Points in Accordance.

Bear out Cave. Lower the body, intending to sit. Dragon

Bends: The shoulders roll over to exchange Yin and Yang. The waist leads the shoulders.

The two hands correspond. Deliver the energy to the middle fingers in order to move forcefully. Move both hands at the same time. The front hand thrusts backward as if putting the sword into the scabbard. The back hand thrusts forward as far as possible, the index finger pointing to the opponent. Both elbows overlap on the navel to form the shape of scissors, with the elbows as the axis. Tuck the chest and stretch the back. The hands follow the shoulders. The original front shoulder now becomes the back one. The original back shoulder now becomes the front one.

Si Ba (Tearing Hold)

1. Use Draw a Bow or Prop Pole, Clip and Cut or Three Points Align as postures. Open the chest. Push the elbows outward in opposite directions with Roc Elbows. The hands split in front of the stomach. The forearm of the front hand is vertical to the ground, the thumb pointing inward. The back hand pushed downward and backward, the elbow bending inward about 150°, the thumb by the hip (The area normally is used for injections). The hands follow the elbows and push outward in opposite directions. Strike with the front hand and back elbow.

Lean the body forward slightly. Lower the body intending to sit.

內要提，外要隨，起要橫，落要順；打要遠，氣要催。

盧式心意六合拳入門

1

2

4

3

5

6

7

8

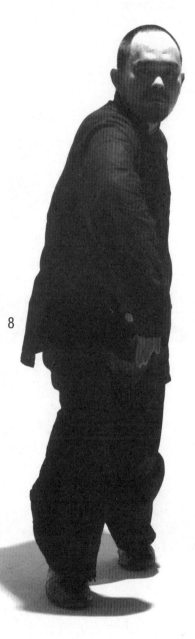

十四、過地風（樁功、單邊）

學習模仿雞在欺鬥過程中出腳時的動作模樣。一是養成習慣性，在進步時抬腳傷人；二是訓練腳頭的抗擊打能力。後腿蹬前腿起，起若疾風掃地，貼地而前，搓而上。有樁打拳時也分單樁單腿、雙樁雙腿。單樁單腿打拳時，在支撐腿的大腿根與小腹的交界處夾一穀物或紙片，單重，搓腳。雙樁雙腿在打拳時手腳如繫一線，同起同落，轉身，搓腳。

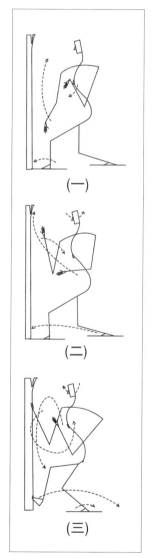

（一）

（二）

（三）

熊舔把：開弓放箭式、夾剪之式、三尖照。

雙把合二為一，把有前後之分，同時出把，前把（左把）翻而上抬，把心朝上，端而上，把動而肘不動，肘不離脇，豎把而止，中指朝上，把心朝裡，把與頭合，有舔掌之意；後把折腕下塌，把心朝下，止於襠上，食指罩敵。

身有坐意，沉而下。寸步。

過地風：拳為沖天炮，腳為過地風。

龍折身：雙膀一陰翻一陽。把隨身走，前把內塌而落，鵬肘，過心過臍，止於襠前，屈肘（大於90度角，小於150度角），把心朝下，有按埋之意，下把內翻、成拳，衝天而上，止於鼻高，拳背朝外。

過步 —— 過地風。過地風沾實有二：一為沾實腳前掌。腳起要翻，翻有上意，折腕、屈膝，前腳掌沾實。二為大腳趾沾實。腳起平搓而去。如趟地上之露水，屈膝，平腳，大腳趾沾實。

原路返回，週而復始。

14. Guo Di Feng（Wind Over the Ground）（Stance）

Imitate a chicken's fighting. First, get used to attacking while walking. Second, train the foot to bear the strike. Push the ground with the back foot and lift the front foot. Step forward, sliding and rubbing over the floor, as a fast wind sweeps the ground. Stance includes Single Stance Single Leg and Double Stance Double Leg. While practicing Single Stance Single Leg, imagine that there is a grass or a piece of paper under the armpit, single side supports, rub the foot over the floor. While practicing Double Stance Double Leg, imagine that feet and hands are tied by a thread, lifting and falling at the same time. Turn the body and rub feet over the floor.

Xiong Tian Ba (Bear Licking its Claw)

Use Draw a Bow or Prop Pole, Clip and Cut or Three Points in Accordance as postures.

Hands correspond. One hand is before the other. Move both hands at the same time. Raise the front hand and turn the palm to face up. Then keep the elbow beside the ribs, and raise the hand only until the fingers point up. The palm is fac-ing inward, the hand close to the head, with intention of licking the hand. Bend the wrist of the back hand, the palm facing downward, and stop it in front of the crotch. The index finger is pointing to the opponent.

Lower the body intending to sit.

Over Step.

Guo Di Feng (Wind over the Ground): Hand movement, punch upward. The foot moves like wind over the ground.

Long Zhe Shen (Dragon Bends): The shoulders roll over to exchange Yin and Yang. Hands follow the body. The front hand falls to the crotch, bending the arm greater than $90°$, less than $150°$, palm facing downward with intention of pressing and covering. Turn the lower hand inward and change it into a fist, punching upward to nose level. The back of the hand faces out.

Over step and Wind over the Ground. There are two ways to practice Wind over the Ground. One is to stamp the forefoot on the ground. Raise the foot with toes pointing up, bending the ankle and the knee. Focus on the forefoot. The other is stamping on the ground with the toe. Raise the foot and move as if wiping dew from the floor. Bend the knee, stretch the foot, focusing on the big toe.

1 2

3 4

盧式心意六合拳入門

5

6

7

8

十五、鯉魚打挺（椿功）

鯉魚打挺（椿功）

　　盧式心意拳有十個大形，若干個小形，這一把拳是學習模仿魚在水裡游的過程中打挺換向時的動作模樣，突然、無徵兆。以前腳為圓心，轉胯，側身，沾實於身體一側的肩、脇、胯，瞬間實俯、拔骨、騰膜、伸筋。選擇椿時要當心，以平直、粗壯為宜。

　　1. 開弓放箭式、牮杆之式、虎抱頭式、貓洗臉式、扶劍把式與劍入鞘式（手形）都可與配合使用。

　　2. 龍折身，雙膀一陰翻一陽，身有起落，旋轉（身法）。

　　3. 同時沾實於身體同側的膀、肋、胯三個部位，練習內臟抗擊打能力，整體撞擊力。

　　4. 過步。

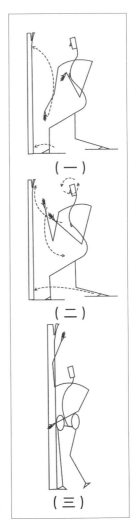

（一）

（二）

（三）

鯉魚打挺（單邊）

熊出洞下式：

　　1. 寸步，長身而前，雙把合而

為一，前把抬而前掛，後把抬而上護。

2. 過步，龍折身，雙膀一陰翻一陽，把隨膀翻，雙把裏實而不露，沾實於雙膀一陰翻一陽的過程中。

3. 原路返回，調邊，週而復始。

15. Li Yu Da Ting (Carp Jump) (Stance)

There are 10 big forms, which include many small shapes in Lu Style Xinyi. This movement is used to imitate carp swimming or jumping to change the direction in the water, suddenly with no premonition. Use the front foot as the centre of the circle, turn the hip, sideways the body. One side of the body, shoulder and hip are solid. At the moment, lean forward and stretch the bones, membranes and tendons.

Choose a straight and strong pole to practice it carefully.

1. Use postures: Draw a Bow, Prop Pole, Tiger Embraces His Head, Cat Washes His Face, Touch the grip of the sword, or Sword Out of the Scabbard (hand posture).

2. Dragon Bends. The shoulders roll over to exchange Yin and Yang. Raise or lower the body, or turn.

3. Focus on the shoulder, ribs and hip on the same side. Improve the strength of striking and defense.

4. Over Step,

Li Yu Da Ting (Carp Jump) (single side)

Xiong Chu Dong (Bear Exits its Den)

1. Inch Step. Move forward straight and forcefully. The front hand parries in front. The back hand parries over the head.

2. Over step and Dragon Bends. The shoulders roll over to exchange Yin and Yang. The hands follow the body. Focus on the hands, but hide the intention.

3. Repeat above movement in the opposite direction.

盧
式
心
意
・
動
作

出手不打臉定是藝兒淺，抬腳不踢襠定是個二貨商。

盧式心意六合拳入門

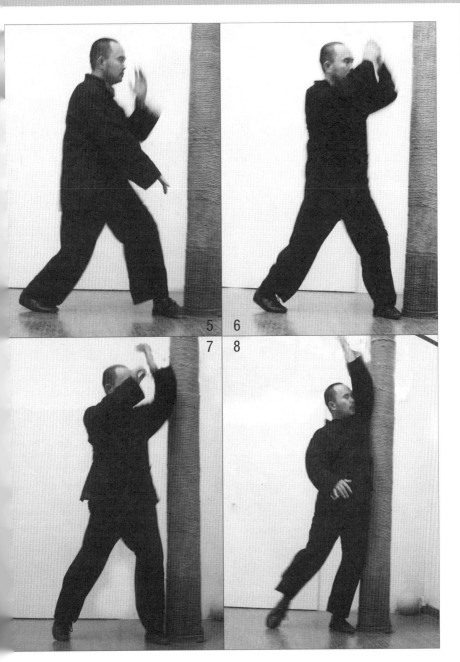

5 6
7 8

十六、狸貓上樹（椿功）

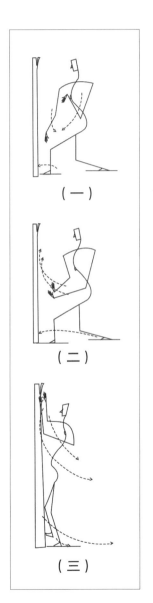

（一）

（二）

（三）

　　盧式心意拳有十個大形，若干個小形，這一把拳是學習模仿貓由地面上樹的過程中瞬間身形變換時的動作模樣，突然、無徵兆。長身而起，雙把搓而上，沾實於身體正面的腹、身體一側的膝和腳。瞬間實俯、拔骨、騰膜、伸筋。選擇椿時要當心，以平直、粗壯為宜。

　　1. 開弓放箭式、牮杆之式、雙虎抱頭式。

　　2. 龍折身，意如豎碑，身有起落（身法）。

　　3. 同時沾實於腹、身體一側的膝、腳三個部位。練習內臟抗擊打能力，鼓實之力。

　　4. 過步。

狸貓上樹（單邊）

熊出洞下式：

　　1. 寸步，長身而前，雙把合

而為一上挫，虎口暗合，止於鼻高。

2. 過步，龍折身，意如豎碑，雙把分而外掛，掛而裏，雙把裏實而不露，沾實於龍折身，意如豎碑的過程中。

3. 原路返回，週而復始。

16. Li Mao Shang Shu（Palm Cat Climbs a Tree）（Stance）

There are 10 big forms, which include many small shapes in Lu Style Xinyi. This movement is used to imitate a palm cat climbing a tree from the ground, shapes changing suddenly with no premonition. Swell the body and stand up. Both hands climb upward. Abdomen in the front of the body, a knee and foot at the same side are solid. At the moment, lean forward and stretch the bones, membranes and tendons. Choose a straight and strong pole to practice it carefully.

Palm Cat Climbs a Tree (Stance) (Li Mao Shang Shu)

1. Use postures：Draw a Bow, Prop Pole, or Tiger Embraces His Head.

2. Dragon Bends. The mind is determined like an upright stone tablet. Raise or lower the body.

3. Focus on the stomach, knee and foot on the same side. Improve the strength of offense and defense.

4. Over Step, Li Mao Shang Shu（Palm cat Climbs a Tree）
（One Side）.

Xiong Tian Ba （Bear Exits its Den）

1. Inch step. Move forward straight and forcefully. Join the hands together and push upward to nose level. The Tiger Mouths correspond.

2. Over step and Dragon Bends. The mind is determined like an upright stone tablet. Both hands parry and swing outward. Focus on the hands, but hide the intention.

3. Repeat 1 and 2.

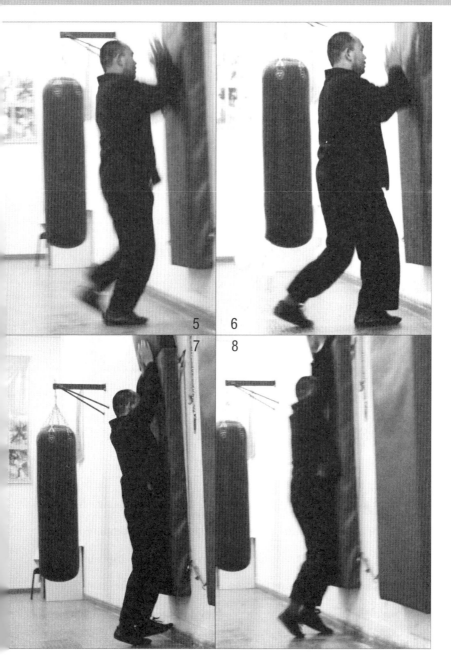

5　6
7　8

盧式心意拳內功：九九之功

任督二脈為陰陽之海，人之脈比於水。故曰：脈之海。任者性也，凡人生育之本。脈起於中極之下，上毛際循腹而上咽喉至承漿而止，此陰脈之海；督脈者為陽脈之經網。尾閭背脊上玉枕、頂、額、鼻柱、人中到上橋止，為陽脈之海。

《金丹秘訣》曰：一擦一兜左右換手，九九之功，真陽不走。戌亥二時（戌時：晚上7：00至9：00，亥時：晚上9：00至11：00），為陰盛陽衰時，一手兜外陽，一手擦臍下（丹田），左右換手各八十一次，半月精固。

李東垣曰：夜半收心靜坐片時，此生發周身元氣之大要也。

Lu Style Xinyi Neigong（Internal Power）： the top internal power skills

There are many energy streams in the human body. Ren and Du are the major ones, which are like the seas, compared to the others, which are like water. They are also called the seas of Yin and Yang. Ren stream, the sea of Yin is in the front of the body, from the testicle where life comes from, goes up along the abdomen and throat, and stops at the ChengJiang（which is an acupuncture point located at the middle of the chin.) Du stream, the sea of Yan, in the back of the body, starts from coccyx and goes up along the spine, then pass the neck, the top of the head, the forehead, the nose, the Renchong (centre of the upper lip), and stops at Shangqiao (middle of the upper gum).

The trick is used to practice the internal power: one hand holds the testicle (for male), the other rubs the part under navel (Dantian), change hands after 81times at the time of Xu and Hai (pm 7:00~9:00 and pm 9:00~11:00), when Yin in the strongest and Yang in the weakest. The real Yang stays inside. Power will be improved in half month.

Li Dongyuan once said, "Concentrating the mind and sitting in peace at midnight is crucial for stimulating the energy of the body."

歡迎至本公司購買書籍

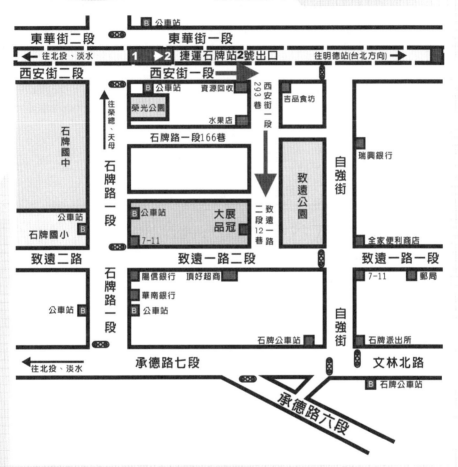

東華街二段   B 公車站   **東華街一段**

← 往北投、淡水   **1 ▶2 捷運石牌站2號出口**   往明德站(台北方向) →

西安街二段   **西安街一段** →

B 公車站   資源回收   西安街一段293巷   吉品食坊

往榮總、天母   榮光公園   水果店

石牌國中   石牌路一段166巷   瑞興銀行

石牌路一段   致遠公園   自強街

公車站 B   B 公車站   大展品冠   二段12巷   致遠一路

石牌國小   7-11   全家便利商店

致遠二路   **致遠一路二段**   **致遠一路一段**

石牌路一段   陽信銀行 頂好超商   7-11   郵局

華南銀行

公車站 B   B 公車站   自強街

石牌公車站   石牌派出所

← 往北投、淡水   **承德路七段**   **文林北路**

B 石牌公車站

承德路六段

建議路線
1. 搭乘捷運・公車
　　淡水線石牌站下車，由石牌捷運站２號出口出站(出站後靠右邊)，沿著捷運高架往台北方向走(往明德站方向)，其街名為西安街，約走100公尺(勿超過紅綠燈)，由西安街一段293巷進來(巷口有一公車站牌，站名為自強街口)，本公司位於致遠公園對面。搭公車者請於石牌站(石牌派出所)下車，走進自強街，遇致遠路口左轉，右手邊第一條巷子即為本社位置。

2. 自行開車或騎車
　　由承德路接石牌路，看到陽信銀行右轉，此條即為致遠一路二段，在遇到自強街(紅綠燈)前的巷子(致遠公園)左轉，即可看到本公司招牌。

國家圖書館出版品預行編目資料

盧式心意六合拳入門 ／ 余 江 著
——初版，——臺北市，大展，2016〔民105 .10〕
面；21公分 ——（中英文對照武學；9）
ISBN 978－986－346－129－6（平裝）

1. 拳術 2. 中國

528 .972　　　　　　　　　　　　　105014763

盧式心意六合拳入門 附VCD

著　　者／余　江
責任編輯／王 躍 平
發 行 人／蔡 森 明
出 版 者／大展出版社有限公司
社　　址／台北市北投區（石牌）致遠一路2段12巷1號
電　　話／（02）28236031・28236033・28233123
傳　　眞／（02）28272069
郵政劃撥／01669551
網　　址／www.dah-jaan.com.tw
E - mail ／ service@dah-jaan.com.tw
登 記 證／局版臺業字第2171號
承 印 者／傳興印刷有限公司
裝　　訂／眾友企業公司
排 版 者／弘益電腦排版有限公司
授 權 者／山西科學技術出版社
初版1刷／2016年（民105年）10月
　　　　　　　　　　　　　　　定 價／330元